The Educational Endowment Series

The Developing Law of Endowment Funds: "The Law and the Lore" Revisited

A REPORT TO THE FORD FOUNDATION

by William L. Cary and Craig B. Bright

THE FORD FOUNDATION
320 East 43rd Street, New York, N.Y. 10017

Library of Congress Catalog Card Number: 74-81012
Printed in the United States of America

Contents

Foreword

Five years ago we asked Professor William L. Cary, Dwight Professor of Law at Columbia University, and Mr. Craig B. Bright of the New York law firm, Patterson, Belknap & Webb, to review and prepare a report on the law governing the management of charitable endowment funds. That study, published under the title "The Law and the Lore of Endowment Funds," was one of a series designed to produce new insights and analyses to improve the management of charitable investments generally and college and university endowments specifically.

The 1969 report by Messrs. Cary and Bright was widely distributed and established itself as a document of basic importance to endowment managers, trustees, and legal counselors. In the intervening years, the law has undergone considerable evolution, and we consequently invited Messrs. Cary and Bright to bring their earlier study up to date, giving special emphasis to the most recent legal developments. This new report is the result of that review.

In recent years, the financial strength of American higher education has suffered further erosion, and the need for more effective use of endowment funds continues to be great. While the study represents the views of its authors only and not necessarily those of the Ford Foundation, we believe that it deserves the serious attention of those concerned with the management of endowment funds. We are deeply grateful to Messrs. Cary and Bright for their additional work.

February 1974

McGeorge Bundy

v

Preface

Five years have passed since the publication of our first report to the Ford Foundation, "The Law and the Lore of Endowment Funds." During this period private institutions of higher learning, with regrettably few exceptions, have slipped closer toward fiscal disaster. Informed comments have ranged from pessimism to outright despair.[1] The financial problems of educational institutions, and many other nonprofit organizations, may fairly be described as monumental.

With a fiscal crisis of such proportions, relatively few institutions will be able to free themselves from the prospect of insolvency solely by the more effective use of available resources. Such self-help is nonetheless imperative; for a number of institutions it may mean the margin between survival and closing. The overriding purpose of this report and its predecessor is an examination of the law to determine its effect on the ability of nonprofit organizations to help themselves in the field of endowment management.

We start with a short summary of our first report and then comment on events and developments since its publication. Finally we turn to an extended analysis of practice and the law relating to a subject we touched upon more lightly five years ago—the delegation of investment responsibility.

I

A Summary of *"The Law and the Lore of Endowment Funds"*

The typical investor has almost limitless flexibility in choosing investments for his portfolio. He can take account of safety, current yield, long-range potential, liquidity, volatility, and all other relevant factors in light of his own circumstances and select an investment tailor-made for his needs.

The typical manager of endowment funds historically has felt deprived of such flexibility by the strictures of the law. Faced with pressing and steadily increasing demands for current revenues, endowment managers thought themselves to be foreclosed from consideration of investments with low current yields (dividends, interest and rents), even though such investments might hold the prospect of significantly higher total return (yield plus appreciation). This apparent limitation was based upon the assumption that only the yield of endowment funds may be expended; stated differently, it was assumed that capital gains may not be expended, on the theory that they constitute part of the principal of endowment funds, which must be maintained intact and in perpetuity.

Our first report was devoted in large measure to an analysis of the validity and effects of that assumption. We examined the terms of typical donative instruments, reviewed the relevant statutory and case law, considered the definition and concept of "income" from the points of view of various disciplines, and came to the following conclusions:

(1) Donors of endowment funds have in the past almost never specified whether realized gains must be retained as principal or may be expended as income. Typically, they have simply directed that their gift be added to "endowment," or that it be invested and the "income" used for a specified purpose.

(2) Statutes left the question open in virtually all the states, and the courts have not yet spoken.

(3) Corporate law and trust law both offer solutions, but they are diametrically opposed.

(4) In determining what principles to apply to the solution of the problem, the question is not whether a charitable corporation is the "absolute owner" of its property or merely holds it "in trust." No jurisdiction treats charitable corporations exactly like business corporations or exactly like trusts for all purposes; all jurisdictions apply the principles of corporate law to the solution of some of their problems, and the principles of trust law to the solution of others. The choice of principles depends upon the factual situation before the court.

(5) Where the issue involved is not one of administration, the only clearly discernible judicial trend or attitude is a marked tendency to favor charities in their disputes with others over property, and corporate law or trust law is used less for guidance than to rationalize the desired result.

(6) Where the issue involved is one of administration, particularly financial administration, courts uniformly tend to apply the more flexible principles found in corporate law.

(7) To an ever-increasing extent, dividends are being commuted by our investment community into capital gains. They are treated as interchangeable by economists, accountants, tax lawyers and corporate lawyers. Only under trust law are they considered basically different.

We were thus led to the conclusion that there is no substantial authority under existing law to support the widely held view that the realized gains of endowment funds of educational institutions must be treated as principal. Exhaustive research uncovered no case that either affirmed or denied the legal right of such an institution to determine for itself whether to retain all such gains or to expend a prudent part. We could find no reason why the law should deny educational institutions that flexibility.

If colleges and universities are in fact legally free to treat capital gains as expendable income, it may logically be asked whether such expenditure must be limited to realized appreciation, or can it be extended to unrealized appreciation as well? To most economists the "realization" of gains and losses is an artificial, almost meaningless concept. Assume that an educational institution holds two securities, each of which is now worth $100. Security "A" originally cost $150, while security "B" cost $50. In terms of economic power the institution is exactly where it was when it purchased the two; it still holds securities worth an aggregate of $200. But depending upon which security it chooses to sell, it will be said to have "realized" a gain or a loss of $50 —even if it immediately repurchases the security it sold. Economists emphasize that in reality the institution is neither better nor worse off for having gone through the exercise of selling and buying back, and the logic of their position seems unassailable. Such reasoning seems especially cogent when applied to educational institutions, which are tax-exempt.

But in our report we were discussing the law as it exists and as it is likely to find expression in the judicial opinions of the foreseeable future. It is enough to ask the courts to take one major step within the bounds of traditional thinking. To depart from the concept of realization would be to cast tradition completely aside. In light of this, we considered it to be quite unlikely that a court today would regard the unrealized appreciation of an endowment fund as expendable income, and we therefore limited our discussion to the proper classification of realized gains alone.*

We believe that the courts not only should, but eventually will, hold that the realized appreciation of endowment funds constitutes income. They may also hold that such appreciation can be spent in full, but it seems to us more likely that by application of the prudent man rule certain safeguards will be imposed to govern the expenditure. One of the safeguards most likely to commend itself to the courts relates to

---

*A legislature enjoys considerably more latitude in this regard than a court. The Uniform Management of Institutional Funds Act, which has now been adopted in more than a dozen states, specifically allows the expenditure of unrealized appreciation. See pp. 12-13, *infra*.

inflation. The prudent man concerned with the safety of his capital would retain enough of his realized gains to compensate for losses due to inflation, and it seems logical to assume that most administrators of college and university endowment funds would deem it prudent to do the same. Another area of concern relates to losses. Prudence would call for the establishment of reserves from gains realized in one year which could be drawn upon to absorb losses which may be realized in the next.

Means of Classifying Realized Gains as Income

Although we concluded that it would be desirable for educational institutions to have the flexibility in their investment planning that would flow from classifying realized gains as income, and that neither the terms of typical donative instruments nor the law as it now exists would bar such a classification, we nevertheless recognized that it had been the traditional practice of most cautious administrators of endowment funds to classify realized gains as principal. To bring about a change in that practice would require affirmative action. In this respect we recommended consideration of a suit for a declaratory judgment, legislation (including promulgation of a proposed model act), the use of quasi-endowment funds,* and greater care in the drafting of future donative instruments.

Although our first report was devoted primarily to a discussion of the proper classification of appreciation of endowment funds, we examined several other topics as well. Our conclusions as to those matters are summarized below.

Permissible Investments

Donors, legislatures, and the common law alike, have as a rule given educational institutions wide discretion in the choice of investments.

*Consideration should be given as well to a careful study of donative instruments to make certain that the endowment funds of the institution in question are properly classified. For purposes of our initial report we examined 462 instruments governing individual funds held by a cross section of private institutions in the East. We restricted our study to funds that the institutions classified as "pure endowment"; that is, those funds the principal of which the institutions considered themselves to be legally barred from spending. Nevertheless, we discovered that approximately 22% of the instruments studied (both in number of instruments and dollar amount of the funds involved) contained no legal prohibition whatsoever against spending principal. Many explicitly authorized the institutions to expend principal in their discretion. This suggests that at least some of the restrictions that supposedly fetter the free exercise of discretion in this area are wholly imaginary, arising from misclassification.

4

The requirement most frequently applied is that the institution invest as a prudent man would invest his own funds for the long term, having in mind both income and the safety of capital. Today capital cannot be considered safe unless its purchasing power is protected.

The Fear of Liability

Neither directors nor trustees are liable under the law for reasonable mistakes of judgment or for failure to foresee events that are not generally anticipated. A trustee may be liable for actual negligence, but directors have not even been held to that standard at common law. As a practical matter the courts require proof of bad faith or gross or willful neglect before imposing personal liability upon directors of business corporations, and the little authority in point indicates that this is true also in respect of directors of charitable corporations.

Delegation of Investment Responsibility

There is nothing in the law to condemn the delegation of investment responsibility to a committee of the board and even to a responsible officer of a charitable corporation. Delegation outside the corporate structure can more easily be questioned, but such delegation should nevertheless be upheld if the corporation retains ultimate control.*

---

*Delegation of investment responsibility is discussed more fully later in this report. See p. 21 *et seq., infra.*

II

Recent Events

Changing Attitudes and Practices

As we pointed out earlier, the financial plight of nonprofit institutions has grown steadily more serious since the publication of our first report. The magnitude of the financial crisis facing colleges, universities, and other nonprofit institutions has inevitably led to a reevaluation of traditional rules and practices. Whether such practices have actually contributed to the crisis may be debated, but it seems self-evident that they have proved inadequate to cope with it.

As an Ohio court noted several years ago,

> "There is nothing more certain in life than change. As a wise man has said: 'New occasions teach new duties; time makes ancient good uncouth.' What is reasonable and helpful today may not remain so with the passing of years. No man can accurately anticipate the needs of the next generation. . . ."[2]

In the case of endowment funds, attention has naturally centered on ways and means of making them more productive, with particular emphasis on maintaining their purchasing power in the face of spiralling inflation.[3] This has led to a marked increase in the use of professional portfolio managers, a phenomenon discussed at greater length later in this report.* It has led as well to widespread acceptance of the basic

---

*See pp. 23 to 25, *infra.*

precepts of the doctrine of "total return"; that is, that the primary goal of investment policy for endowment funds should be the production of maximum long-term return, taking into account appreciation as well as ordinary yield.[4]

Endowment funds are by definition intended to remain in existence in perpetuity. Rules governing expenditures from such funds are designed at least in part to carry out that intent. The proponents of the total return concept do not seek the abolition of such rules. They recognize the need for standards that will enable their institutions to continue their programs on existing levels for the indefinite future.[5] Their principal quarrel with the traditional trust rule, which would limit expenditures to dividends and interest, is that it has failed in a number of instances to safeguard the continued existence of the endowment funds to which it has been applied.[6]

The traditional trust rule developed during an era of relatively stable investment returns and stable price levels; half a century ago an income beneficiary could reasonably expect to receive annually about 5% on the principal of a trust, and the remainderman could count on receiving the principal with little appreciation or loss.[7] Loss or diminution of principal was the primary, if remote, danger facing the trust, and the prudent trustee guarded against that danger.[8] In today's economy the risk of loss of purchasing power through the relentless onslaught of inflation is the most serious threat to any investment portfolio, and no trustee can truly be considered prudent unless he takes that threat into account. An increasing number of commentators have voiced the opinion that trustees should be held pecuniarily liable for failure to protect their trusts against inflation.[9] We belive that it is only a question of time until the courts impose such a liability.

As one university treasurer has noted, under the best of circumstances "adherence to the Yield standard [that is, the traditional trust rule] will only by coincidence strike the correct balance between the present and the future."[10] By his choice of investments, a portfolio manager today can produce, with relative ease, yields that vary from less than 1% annually to over 8%. Under such circumstances a principal-income dichotomy becomes almost meaningless, even for traditional trusts. In the words of one commentator:

> "It is submitted that there should be some better method for dividing the benefits of a trust fund than by the arbitrary labels

8

of principal and income which can be varied so greatly by a trustee that they have little meaning in terms of dollars. It is submitted that the investment aim of a trustee should be to produce the greatest total of principal, income and appreciation . . . . This greater single fund could then be divided between the life tenant and the remainderman to their mutual advantage, in a manner determined by the testator or grantor."[11]

Similarly, in an incisive article in which he questioned the validity of the traditional trust rule and urged its abandonment, a noted accountant posed the question as follows:

"Prudence after all is still prudence, no matter how you define principal and income. What I am suggesting is that the rules have placed artificial restrictions on the investment policy followed by institutions, which on the whole have prevented them from sharing in a great measure the prosperity the country has been enjoying for the past twenty years. If this is true, then shouldn't the rules be scrapped?"[12]

Such views have found a marked acceptance among nonprofit organizations. In the past few years such prestigious institutions as Dartmouth, Princeton, Smith, the University of Rochester, and the Smithsonian Institution have followed Cornell, Yale, and the University of Chicago in adopting some form of the total return concept. Dramatic as such notable conversions may be, however, the most remarkable statistic about the change is the breadth of its acceptance. In 1971 Louis Harris and Associates, Inc. conducted a survey of 660 nonprofit institutions, each with an endowment having a market value of $5,000,000 or more (referred to hereinafter as the "Harris Survey").[13] Of the group, 58% approved the total return concept; among the 214 colleges and universities within the group, 70% approved it and 24% opposed.[14]

The approving institutions favored not only the investment goal of total return but, specifically, they favored its practical concomitant—the right of the institution to appropriate capital gains for expenditure in an amount sufficient to compensate for the reduction in yield attendant upon investing for growth as well as current return.[15]

In preparation for this report we polled a large number of institutions of higher learning and charitable foundations in the United States. Of these, 383 colleges and universities and 66 foundations furnished information about their financial practices.* Forty per cent of the responding educational institutions and 30% of the responding foundations now include proportionately more growth stocks in their portfolios than they did three years ago. Sixty-two per cent of the officers responding on behalf of educational institutions and 48% of those responding for foundations now believe that it is legal to spend capital gains from endowment funds which do not specifically prohibit it, although the funds do require principal to be maintained as endowment or in perpetuity.** Twenty-five per cent of those responding for colleges and universities and 5% of those responding for foundations had changed their opinions within the past three years about the legality of spending capital gains.

In an effort to attain the flexibility necessary to permit the expenditure of capital gains, 84% of the colleges and universities in the Harris Survey had undertaken a careful review of each of their donative instruments in order to ascertain and analyze the specific restrictions imposed upon their endowment funds.[16] As our own survey indicates, a number of institutions have decided that the traditional trust rule simply does not govern expenditures from endowment funds.

The questioning and reevaluation that led to widespread acceptance and adoption of the total return concept within the past few years have caused a reevaluation of traditional accounting theories, as well. The National Association of College and University Business Officers ("NACUBO"), for years a stalwart defender of the traditional practice of treating capital gains as additions to principal, has now taken the lead in advocating the modification of accounting practice to accommodate the total return concept. According to NACUBO, *College and University Business Administration,* the leading manual on proper accounting treatment for the endowment funds of educational institutions, is being revised to provide for that accommodation.[17] Publication of the revision is tentatively scheduled for mid-1974.

---

*The responding colleges and universities included 181 with endowments having a market value of $3,000,000 or more as of June 30, 1971 and 157 with endowments having a market value of less than $3,000,000 as of that date; 45 gave incomplete answers or had no endowment. There was no significant difference based upon endowment value in the responses of educational institutions, with respect to the data summarized in this report. The responding foundations have endowments which had an aggregate market value in excess of $5.5 billion as of June 30, 1971. Those foundations with endowments of less than $3,000,000 were too few in number to be statistically significant as a group.

**When representatives of educational institutions were asked an identical question in 1968 in connection with a survey we conducted for purposes of our first report, 58% of those who expressed opinions believed that it would be illegal to spend such gains.

Another notable result of the effort to increase the productivity of endowment funds has been the activation of The Common Fund for Nonprofit Organizations. In the past, institutions with relatively small endowment funds have found it exceedingly difficult to obtain competent investment advice. Even though their endowments are in many cases comparatively more important to such institutions than they are to larger, more solvent organizations, the smaller institutions have simply lacked the resources to pay the fees demanded by top flight investment advisers. The Common Fund attempts to solve that problem for educational institutions by providing a vehicle through which they can pool their funds for investing.*

Participating institutions may elect one of four alternative plans for receiving payments with respect to their investments. More than half have chosen to receive an annual return of 5% of the average market value of the investment.** Units of participation are sold to make up the difference between the amount of dividends and interest received on the investment and the 5% payout. Under the traditional trust rule this would of course represent an invasion of "principal."

Investments in the Fund depart from traditional trust precepts in several other respects as well. Investment decisions are delegated by participating institutions to the Fund, and by the Fund itself to its four professional investment advisers. Investments are commingled in a common fund, and at least in some jurisdictions investments in the Fund would be considered improper for trustees under formal trusts. By nevertheless investing in the Fund, institutions from 42 states, the District of Columbia, and two foreign countries have in effect testified to their belief that such precepts are inapplicable to them.***

---

*Participation in the Fund is open only to nonprofit colleges, universities, and independent schools. The minimum investment that will be accepted from a participating institution is $100,000, and the maximum is $10,000,000.

Organization costs and operating expenses of the Fund through October 1973 were reimbursed or underwritten by the Ford Foundation. The Fund's exemption from federal income taxation has been conditioned in the past upon the continuance of some such support; the exemption would have been lost if participating members had underwritten or paid for a substantial portion of the Fund's operating expenses. The Internal Revenue Service has issued a clarification of its exemption ruling, which will in effect permit the Fund to be reimbursed by its members for operating expenses for an interim period of about four months. As this report goes to press, the Fund is seeking a longer-term solution, either through special legislation or registration of the Fund under the Investment Company Act of 1940.

**The other plans provide respectively for (i) a fixed rate of return other than 5%, (ii) a payout consisting solely of yield (interest and dividends earned on the investment), or (iii) accumulation of all earnings without payout.

***It should be noted, however, that legislation has been enacted in at least three states specifically for the purpose of resolving any doubts about the legality of investments in the Fund.[18] One such statute, from California, is discussed later in this report. See p. 17, *infra*.

Statutory Developments

The change over the past several years in attitudes and practices relating to endowment funds has found its clearest reflection in proposed legislation. Of the statutes that have been adopted or proposed, the most important is the Uniform Management of Institutional Funds Act, which was approved in August 1972 by the National Conference of Commissioners on Uniform State Laws and recommended by the Conference for enactment in all states.*

The Uniform Act permits the governing board of an institution to which it applies to appropriate for expenditure, for the uses and purposes for which the institution's endowment fund is established, so much of the net appreciation, both realized and unrealized, in the fair value of the assets of the fund as is prudent under a specified standard.[19] This would not apply if the applicable gift instrument indicated the donor's intention that net appreciation should not be expended, but such a restriction would not be implied from a designation of the gift as an endowment, or from a direction "to use only income" or "to preserve the principal intact." This rule of construction applies to all gift instruments, regardless of whether they were executed or became effective before or after the effective date of the Act.[20]**

The constitutionality of applying the Uniform Act to preexisting endowment funds was affirmed by the Supreme Court of New Hampshire in an advisory opinion to the State Senate in June 1973.[22]***

The Act sets the following standard of conduct for members of the governing boards of institutions to which it applies:

> "[M]embers of a governing board shall exercise ordinary business care and prudence under the facts and circumstances prevailing at the time of the action or decision. In so doing they shall consider

---

*The Act had been drafted over a two-year period by a committee chaired by George R. Hooper of Chicago. Reporters for the Act were John C. O'Byrne, now Dean of Northeastern University School of Law, and William M. McGovern of the University of California at Los Angeles School of Law.

**The California version of the Act attempts to differentiate between gift instruments in effect prior to the effective date of the statute and those becoming effective thereafter. For preexisting instruments, a restriction on the expenditure of net appreciation "need not" be implied from the use of words such as "endowment"; for post-effective instruments, such a restriction "may not" be implied from such usage.[21] The distinction seems to us to be an unfortunate and meaningless departure from the Uniform Act.

***A similar conclusion was reached by courts that considered the constitutionality of applying the Uniform Principal and Interest Act to preexisting trusts, even though it altered prior rules for allocating earnings between "principal" and "income."[23]

12

long and short term needs of the institution in carrying out its
educational, religious, charitable, or other eleemosynary purposes,
its present and anticipated financial requirements, expected total
return on its investments, price level trends, and general economic
conditions."[24]*

The standard was derived in part from Proposed Treasury Regulations
§ 53.4944-1(a)(2) dealing with the investment responsibility of managers of private foundations.**

Governing boards are given broad powers under the Act in the
selection of investments,[26] and their power to delegate investment
authority is specified in broad terms.[27] Finally, the Act permits the
governing board, with the written consent of the donor, to release in
whole or in part a restriction imposed by the applicable gift instrument
on the use or investment of an institutional fund.[28] If the donor is
unavailable or cannot be identified, an appropriate court, upon application by the governing board and notice to the state's attorney general,
may order the full or partial release of such a restriction upon a finding
that it is obsolete, inappropriate or impracticable.[29]

The Act has already been enacted into law in a number of states,
including California,[30] Colorado, [31] Connecticut,[32] Illinois,[33] Kansas,[34]
Maine,[35] Maryland,[36] Minnesota,[37] New Hampshire,[38] Tennessee,[39]
Vermont,[40] Virginia,[41] and Washington.[42] Bills to enact it are pending
before the legislatures of a number of others, including Massachusetts,[43]
Michigan,[44] Missouri,[45] New Jersey,[46] Ohio,[47] and Wisconsin.[48]

An earlier draft of the Uniform Act formed the basis for a statute
that became effective in Rhode Island on May 3, 1972.[49] However,
the Rhode Island version contains several aberrations that no draft of
the Uniform Act ever embraced. The primary difference lies in the
definition of "historic dollar value." Both the Uniform Act and the
Rhode Island variation define the term as the value in dollars of an
endowment fund at the time it became one, plus the value in dollars of
subsequent additions as of the time they are made.[50] The Rhode Island
version, however, provides for the adjustment of historic dollar value
from time to time to reflect changes in the purchasing power of the

---

*The California version of the Act substitutes the vaguer, less meaningful standard of "the
judgment, care and prudence, under the circumstances then prevailing, which men of discretion and intelligence exercise in the management of their affairs."[25]
**The Regulations were promulgated in final form and became effective on December 28, 1972.

fund. With respect to funds in existence at the time the act was passed, "historic dollar value" is their value in dollars at *that* time, plus the value in dollars of subsequent additions as of the time they are made.* The result is to deprive the institutions to which the legislation applies of a fair measure of the flexibility it was designed to give them.**

In our first report we suggested that inflation be taken into account when appreciation is appropriated for current expenditure. It seems to us, however, that this can most appropriately be done when the *prudence* of the appropriation is considered. By grafting the concept onto the statutory definition of historic dollar value, the Rhode Island legislators have made it unnecessarily difficult for institutions to determine with accuracy the amount of appreciation actually represented in their endowment funds.

New York's Not-for-Profit Corporation Law[52] was the forerunner of statutes dealing with the total return concept. Although as originally enacted it did not apply to educational institutions, it has been amended effective as of September 1, 1973 to apply to them as well.[53] It provides that with respect to any direction relating to principal or interest, in the absence of specific provision to the contrary in a governing instrument, income from the institution's assets

> "may include so much of the realized appreciation of principal as the board may deem prudent, provided that the amount or fair value of the principal of such assets as of the end of the fiscal year in which appreciation so allocated to income was realized, after giving effect to such allocation, shall be not less than the amount or fair value of such assets at the time they were originally received by the corporation. The fair value of such assets may be determined in such manner as the board shall deem appropriate."[54]

It seems regrettable that the legislature saw fit to require the realiza-

---

*Both the Uniform Act and the Rhode Island variation apply to gift instruments executed or in effect before, as well as after, the effective date of the statute. The application to pre-existing instruments is to a large extent nullified by the Rhode Island version.

**Another difference between the Uniform Act and the Rhode Island variation lies in their respective approaches to the release of restrictions imposed by gift instruments on the use or investment of an institutional fund. In addition to release by consent of the donor or by order of a court if he is unavailable, as the Uniform Act allows, Rhode Island permits the state's attorney general to release a restriction if the donor is unavailable or cannot be identified. Further, under the Rhode Island version a court is permitted to order a release even if the donor is living and identifiable (but only on notice to him and the attorney general), and may do so upon a showing that the restriction is obsolete, inappropriate, impracticable or merely "not in keeping with the purposes of the institution."[51]

tion of appreciation prior to its appropriation as income. As we pointed out in our first report, the "realization" of gains and losses is an artificial, almost meaningless concept, particularly for an institution that is not subject to taxation on its income.[55] Gains can be "realized" when the total dollar value of an endowment is considerably less than it was at its inception, just as losses can be "realized" even though the entire portfolio has appreciated substantially in value. The requirement that appreciation be realized prior to its appropriation as income will of necessity impose artificial strictures on investment managers in the selection of portfolio securities for retention or liquidation. Instead of a selection based solely on the investment worth of the securities at the time of the selection, the extraneous happenstance of their individual appreciation or decline from original cost may dictate a completely different decision.

At least two other provisions of the New York statute are open to question. The statute provides that after giving effect to an allocation of realized appreciation to income, the fair value of the assets of the fund as of the end of the fiscal year in which the appreciation was *realized* cannot be less than their value when originally received by the institution. What of appreciation realized in one year, when the test could be met, but which is not appropriated to income until several years thereafter, at a time when the value of assets of the fund may have plummeted far below their original value? It could be argued that the test should in logic be applied at the time or year of appropriation, not realization. However, such a requirement could presumably be met by a yearly appropriation to an income reserve of all appreciation realized during the year; the reserve could then be expended over the years as the need arises. If this is true a change in the statute would be pointless; it would merely force the institution to engage in accounting maneuvers in order to do what the statute now allows it to do directly. A more realistic alternative would be to apply the test at the time or year of expenditure, rather than of realization or appropriation. But it should be recognized that if this is done some institutions might be induced to spend funds currently when they would otherwise be husbanded, because a delay in expenditure, coupled with a decline in the market value of the fund, might "freeze" appreciation that could have been spent when realized.

The remaining ambiguity of the New York statute arises from an attempt to limit its retroactive effect. The statute applies to assets received before its effective date, as well as to those received thereafter,

> "except that, with respect to assets held at the time when this chapter takes effect, if the corporation has theretofore treated realized appreciation as principal, the amount of such past realized appreciation that may thereafter be transferred to income in any one year shall not exceed twenty per cent of the total."[56]

The difficulty is that there is no clear antecedent for "such past realized appreciation." Probably the legislature meant to refer to appreciation realized prior to the effective date of the act, and we believe that the proviso should be so interpreted. However, it could also be read as applying to appreciation of prior-held assets that is realized after the effective date but not appropriated to income until some time thereafter.

Pennsylvania has enacted an extensively revised Nonprofit Corporation Law, which became effective on February 13, 1973. It provides that

> "so much of the net realized capital gains as of the end of any fiscal year of the corporation as the directors or other body shall, within four months after the end of such year, in their sole discretion, allocate to income for such fiscal year shall be deemed income."[57]

However, the amount so allocated, when added to all other income derived by the corporation from the same assets during the fiscal year in question, shall not exceed 9% of the market value (as of the end of that fiscal year) of the principal of such assets remaining after the allocation.[58] The statute applies to assets received before the effective date of the statute and held at that date, to assets received thereafter and to reinvestments of all such assets.[59] The gains that are subject to allocation are all realized capital gains, less all realized capital losses, from the inception of the fund.[60]

Another provision of the Pennsylvania law permits a nonprofit corporation to transfer endowment funds to a corporate trustee,* thus relieving the governing board of the nonprofit corporation from all liability for the administration of the funds so transferred while they are administered by the corporate trustee.[61] The income to be paid over to the nonprofit corporation may include so much of the realized

---

*The trustee must be a Pennsylvania bank or trust company or a national banking association with fiduciary powers that has its principal offices in Pennsylvania.

appreciation as its governing board may deem prudent.[62] Interestingly, the amount of appreciation that can be appropriated to income is limited only by the test of prudence; appropriation is not restricted to a percentage of the market value of the fund, as it is in the case of an endowment fund administered by the governing board itself.

A North Carolina statute that became effective on July 1, 1972 contains the following provision with respect to the endowment funds of constituent institutions of the University of North Carolina:

> "The principal of said endowment fund shall be kept intact and only the income therefrom may be expended. The trustees of the endowment fund shall determine what is income and what is principal."[63]

On July 19, 1972 the governor of California signed into law a bill that was intended to enable educational institutions in California to invest their endowment funds in The Common Fund for Nonprofit Organizations. It permits such institutions to receive annual distributions in amounts up to 10% of the funds so invested and to expend them currently,

> ". . . notwithstanding the provisions of any general or special law characterizing such distribution, or any part thereof, as principal or income; provided, that, in the case of funds or property invested as fiduciary, such expenditure is not prohibited by the wording of the will, deed or other instrument creating such fiduciary relationship. No such prohibition of expenditure shall be deemed to exist solely because a will, deed or other such instrument, whether executed or in effect before or after the effective date of this section, directs or authorizes the use of only the 'income,' or 'interest,' or 'dividends,' or 'rents, issues or profits,' or contains words of similar import."[64]

The quoted words were derived from an early draft of the Uniform Management of Institutional Funds Act.

At the request of Princeton University and other members of the New Jersey Independent Colleges Association, New Jersey enacted an Educational Endowment Management Act effective July 1, 1971. In order to encourage educational institutions to attain the highest income from their endowments, the Act permits such institutions to adopt a plan for allocating to their current operating expenses endowment pool income "in excess of the actual interest, dividends, income, rents, is-

17

sues and profits yielded or earned by the endowment pool."[65] The plan need not conform to the New Jersey Principal and Income Act "or any other statute or decisional law appertaining to the distribution of income, dividends, capital gains realized or unrealized, or other increments of value as between a life or other tenant and remainderman in a trust estate."[66]

Before the plan can become effective it must have received the approval of the Superior Court of New Jersey in a civil action instituted by the institution, to which the Attorney General has been made a party.[67] A statutory rule of construction provides that "income" as defined in such a plan will be deemed to satisfy directions in a gift instrument which limit the institution to the use of only the "income" or "interest" or "dividends" or "rents, issues or profits" of the gift, unless the instrument contains an express provision to the contrary.[68] The Uniform Management of Institutional Funds Act contains a similar rule of construction.*

A Summary of Recent Events Relating to Total Return

The worsening financial plight of nonprofit institutions has led to an increasingly widespread acceptance of the basic precepts of the doctrine of total return; that is, that the primary goal of investment policy for endowments should be the production of maximum long-term revenue, taking into account appreciation as well as ordinary yield.

Seventy per cent of the large group of college and university officers interviewed for an extensive survey conducted by Louis Harris and Associates, Inc. approved the total return concept and favored the right of the institution to appropriate capital gains for expenditure in an amount sufficient to compensate for the reduction in yield attendant upon investing for growth as well as current income.

The National Association of College and University Business Officers has taken the lead in demanding a change in accounting principles to accommodate the total return concept.

Two hundred seventy-five institutions have invested in The Common Fund for Nonprofit Organizations, and over half of these have elected to receive payments from the Fund on a total return basis.

---

*See p. 12, *supra*.

The acceptance of the total return concept has been reflected most clearly in legislation. Statutes have been enacted in a number of states to accommodate total return, and the National Conference of Commissioners on Uniform State Laws has recommended legislative approval of the concept in all states through the adoption of the Uniform Management of Institutional Funds Act.

III

Delegation of Investment Responsibility

In this section we discuss the delegation by nonprofit institutions of the responsibility for making investment decisions relating to their funds. First we examine the importance of delegation to the effective management of endowments. Then we discuss the extent to which institutions do in fact delegate. We then examine the law relating to the right of nonprofit institutions to delegate investment decisions, and finally we suggest guidelines and safeguards which might be useful in accommodating practice to the law.

The Significance of Delegation as a Management Tool

In view of the enormous size of some university and foundation endowment funds, the vital importance of even small endowments, the intricacies of the market, and the complexities of the economy, it seems obvious that management of the funds calls for professional skill and careful, day-to-day attention.[69] The directors of most nonprofit institutions lack both the experience and the time to provide personally that type of management.

Directors are chosen for a variety of reasons, few of which have

21

anything to do with expertise in portfolio management.[70] Once elected they face a myriad of responsibilities, most of them unrelated to portfolio management.[71] And those responsibilities must be met on a part-time basis by men who are typically fully occupied in other endeavors.[72] The Harris Survey found that 26% of college and university trustees spend one day or less per month working as a trustee; almost two-thirds of the trustees average only two days per month.[73] The survey concluded, understandably, that "boards and trustees are passing judgment [regarding endowment management] on at best a part-time basis—and with not a very high profit at that."[74]

The governing board of an institution is responsible for establishing the institution's ultimate goals and overall policies, and must monitor the performance of the institution's executives and staff. The available time that it can devote to the discharge of that responsibility is of necessity limited. If its time is taken up to any large extent with administrative details, it necessarily follows that the board's ability to do an effective job in the formulation of institutional policies and in overseeing institutional performance will be diminished. As Professor Conard of the University of Michigan Law School observed in discussing the function of a business corporation's board of directors:

> "All that a board can do is indicate general policies and objectives. As the enterprise grows larger, even the policies and objectives become far too numerous for a board to undertake them."[75]

In a volatile market the timing of purchases and sales can be as important as the selection of the securities to be bought or sold, even for long-term investors such as the typical endowment fund.[76] If the "buy-sell decision"* is made by a single investment manager, it can be executed without delay. If it is made instead by vote of a large governing board that convenes infrequently, the institution will lose control over timing, and investment performance may suffer.

Even apart from the pressures of time, most informed commentators believe that a committee is the least effective vehicle for reaching investment decisions.[77] This is not to say that an informed and interested committee cannot serve a valuable, even vital function as a sounding board for an investment manager, and of course the goals and policies

---

*By this we mean the decision to buy or sell a given security.

of an investment program are typically established by the governing board or one of its committees.[78] But if the actual buy-sell decision is left to a committee, the result (in the words of a well-known report to the Ford Foundation by its Advisory Committee on Endowment Management):

> ". . . almost inevitably falls into either a 'consensus' or a "majority' mode of decision-making, and neither is well suited to successful long-term investment. The former normally results in a compromise that has been aptly described as 'the lowest common denominator,' and the latter almost always produces erratic swings in policy due to variations in attendance at successive meetings."[79]

And, as is true of any committee action, the responsibility for poor performance is shared by all members of the committee, and thus is the primary concern of none of them.[80] Individual responsibility and accountability go hand in hand.

It has been said with justification that the mystique of the investment manager can be and has been overemphasized.[81] It is nevertheless true that most informed observers believe that investment management, like most jobs, can best be performed by those who are trained to do it, and who, moreover, have the time and incentive to do it well.

The Extent of Delegation by Educational Institutions

The foregoing considerations have led most educational institutions to the conclusion that investment decisions *must* be delegated, at least to some extent.[82] The comment of the treasurer of a leading university bears repetition:

> ". . . since they [the directors] cannot attend continuously to the administration of this responsibility, there must be a Finance Committee; and since it, too, cannot be in continuous session, it must have a Chairman; and since the Chairmanship is not, and should not be, the whole life work of the Chairman, there must be a professional adviser. Moreover, it is now generally agreed among experts that to achieve the best results the professional adviser must have sufficient competence to assume real responsibility for investment performance, and to lead in regard to transactions. Ordinarily, protracted Committee consideration of particular investments should be unnecessary. Indeed, the best modern portfolio managers cannot be employed on any other basis."[83]

The Harris Survey found that the full governing boards of colleges and universities rarely undertake the actual management of the endowment funds of their institutions. Indeed, in the case of half of the institutions, buy-sell decisions are being made for endowment portfolios by investment managers completely outside the corporate structure of the institution. Only one-third of the colleges and universities manage their entire endowment internally.[84]*

The findings of the Harris Survey are in line with the results of our own poll. In the case of only 3% of the 383 colleges and universities that responded to our questionnaire are buy-sell decisions made by the full governing board of the institution. An external investment manager makes buy-sell decisions for the entire endowment portfolio of 37% of the responding institutions and for part of the portfolio for an additional 16%. In other words, more than half of the institutions (53%) have delegated to managers outside the corporate structure the decision to buy and sell securities for their endowment funds. Where buy-sell decisions are made in whole or in part within the corporate structure, external securities experts regularly make investment recommendations for 65% of the institutions.**

In 65% of the educational institutions for which buy-sell decisions are made by an external investment manager, reports of the decisions are made "promptly" to someone in authority within the institution. In all but 4% of the cases such reports are made at least as often as quarterly. However, reports reach the full governing board "promptly" in only 6% of the cases, again demonstrating the widespread extent of internal delegation among institutions today.***

Some or all of the persons who make the buy-sell decisions for our responding institutions are directly compensated for their work by 58%

---

*An "internally" managed endowment is one for which the investment managers are directors or employees of the institution acting in that capacity. An "externally" managed endowment is one for which the investment managers are independent contractors operating outside the corporate structure of the institution, such as banks, trust companies, and investment advisers.

**Proportionately as many of the 66 charitable foundations that responded to our questionnaire have delegated buy-sell decisions to external investment managers as was true of the responding colleges and universities. Such decisions have been delegated to an external manager for the entire endowment portfolio of 32% of the foundations and for part of the portfolio of an additional 17%, for a total of 49%. Of those foundations that employ internal management, however, a significantly higher percentage (20%) than responding colleges and universities utilize the full governing board to make buy-sell decisions for all (18%) or part (2%) of their portfolio.

***The responses of charitable foundations with respect to the matters discussed in this paragraph were virtually identical to those of the responding colleges and universities.

24

of the colleges and universities and 62% of the foundations. Persons making the buy-sell decisions for 7% of the colleges and universities and 8% of the foundations receive brokerage commissions upon the execution of orders for their endowments. The risk that such an arrangement could lead to unwarranted trading seems obvious.

At least two studies have reached the conclusion that externally managed endowment funds achieve superior results.[85] Although we do not question the accuracy of the reported findings, it may be that they in fact measure the expertise of the managers rather than their classification as "internal" or "external." In the opinion of many observers a full-time professional can achieve superior results whether he works inside or outside of the institution's corporate structure.[86] But while some internally managed funds employ such full-time professionals, many others rely instead on committees of part-time directors. External investment managers, on the other hand, are almost by definition full-time professionals.

The Law Relating to Delegation

(A) IN GENERAL

It can be seen, then, that the directors of educational institutions and charitable foundations almost invariably delegate to others responsibility for the investment of their institutions' endowment funds. The delegates may themselves be directors, as a committee of the whole board, or they may be officers or ordinary employees of the institution. In approximately half of the cases the delegates are investment managers operating completely outside the corporate structure.

We shall examine in some detail the law relating to such delegation, but it can be noted now that in the absence of a controlling statute the legality of delegation of investment decisions by the directors of non-profit corporations may largely depend upon whether they are held to the standards imposed on trustees or to those imposed on corporate directors. As Professor Karst of Ohio State University pointed out:

> "A trustee, private or charitable, is severely limited in delegating his duties to others. Under the prevailing view, for example, he cannot delegate to others the choosing of the trust's investments. By comparison, the director of the business corporation frequently must delegate duties of a highly important and discretionary

25

nature, and of course the necessity of such delegation increases with the size and complexity of the enterprise. Thus the rule has been established that corporate directors may delegate most management duties provided that they retain general supervision over the business. Despite the absence of decisional authority, it has been assumed that the corporate rule generally will be applied to charitable corporations."[87]

The question posed is whether the assumption that corporate law controls is well founded. The answer is of considerably more than academic importance to the directors involved, because a "trustee" who improperly delegates investment responsibility for the assets of the "trust" will generally be held liable as an absolute guarantor against loss. A holding of the Supreme Court of the State of Washington is typical:

> "The authorities seem to be practically harmonious in holding that when a trustee unlawfully delegates and surrenders his discretionary powers to someone else, with reference to the control and management of the trust property, he becomes a guarantor and is responsible for any loss that may have resulted, whether or not such loss can be shown to be the result of the delegation of power; the theory being that it is against public policy for one to delegate powers which have been entrusted to him alone, and that the trustee who has placed the trust property in the hands of others will not, after the property has been lost, be heard to say that the delegation of power was not responsible for the loss and that, if he had performed his duties as the law required, the loss would also have occurred. . . ."[88]

If that standard were applied to the directors of nonprofit corporations, they could find themselves personally liable for such fortuitous and uncontrollable events as a general decline in the stock market, unless they personally made all "buy-sell" decisions for the endowment funds entrusted to their care.

But that is the penalty only for an *improper* delegation. Even under trust law *some* delegation is permissible, and as Lord Hardwicke observed more than two centuries ago:

> ". . . where trustees act by other hands, either from necessity, or conformable to the common usage of mankind, they are not answerable for losses."[89]

That is still the law (assuming proper selection and supervision of the delegate), even though the act of the delegate would have constituted a breach of trust if committed by the trustee himself.[90] The Second Restatement of Trusts spells out the rule in more detail:

> "§ 225. *Liability for Acts of Agents*
> "(1) Except as stated in Subsection (2), the trustee is not liable to the beneficiary for the acts of agents employed by him in the administration of the trust.
> "(2) The trustee is liable to the beneficiary for an act of such an agent which if done by the trustee would constitute a breach of trust, if the trustee
> (a) directs or permits the act of the agent; or
> (b) delegates to the agent the performance of acts which he was under a duty not to delegate; or
> (c) does not use reasonable care in the selection or retention of the agent; or
> (d) does not exercise proper supervision over the conduct of the agent; or
> (e) approves or acquiesces in or conceals the act of the agent; or
> (f) neglects to take proper steps to compel the agent to redress the wrong."[91]

(B) INTERNAL DELEGATION

We have found no substantial authority that would prevent a charitable corporation from delegating investment responsibility for its endowment funds to a committee of its board, or to its officers, or to other responsible employees, subject of course to the overall supervision of the board of directors. With one exception the few authorities in point uphold the right of the corporation to provide for such delegation, and such authorities are supported by both logic and common sense.

In the foregoing section, we discussed generally the application to the directors of nonprofit corporations of trust or corporate principles governing delegation. But it should be clearly recognized that the application of trust principles to the directors would necessarily be based upon a misconception; if anyone is the "trustee" of the typical endowment fund, it is the institution which administers it, not the individual members of the institution's board of directors. Technically, the principle that trustees may not delegate investment responsibility has nothing to do with delegation within a corporate structure, even if the corporation itself were considered to be a technical trustee. In such a case, the trustee itself delegates nothing; it acts through agents, as it

27

must.[92] Professor Scott points out that the underlying reason for the rule against delegation, "the element of reliance upon personal judgment and discretion[,] is wanting in the case of a corporate trustee, since it can act only through its directors, officers and employees and these may change from time to time."[93]* Without reference to investment responsibility, he states that certain acts are of sufficient importance that they must be performed by the directors or by a responsible committee or officer and not by an ordinary employee. This is, of course, true also in the case of a business corporation. It is based on the logical operation of the corporate chain of command and not upon technicalities of trust law. That chain of command should not operate in such a manner as to force part-time, unpaid directors of educational institutions personally to make investment decisions that they lack the time and training to make intelligently.

If the principles of corporate law are applied, the courts should have little difficulty in upholding delegation within the corporate structure, despite the apparent conflict between such delegation and the ancient maxim of Anglo-Saxon law, *delegatus non potest delegare* (that is, a delegate cannot himself delegate). In attempting to reconcile the maxim with the power of corporate directors to delegate managerial functions, early decisions followed the trust approach of distinguishing ministerial tasks from those involving discretion; only the delegation of the former was condoned.[95] When this failed to provide the flexibility that the reality of business life demanded, it was reasoned that there is no violation of the maxim if the directors retain at least "ultimate," as opposed to direct, supervision[96] or do not attempt to delegate "extraordinary powers, which by reasonable standards ought to be exclusively in the province of the board of directors."[97] Others said that the maxim did not apply at all, because corporate directors have original powers derived directly from the state by the act of incorporation, not delegated powers derived from the stockholders.[98] Professor Ballantine felt this approach to be quite unnecessary; for him it was sufficient to observe that directors are general managers with plenary

---

*Although the case involved successor trustees rather than internal delegation, language from an Illinois decision is in point:

> "The rule [against delegation] cannot be applied to the case of a corporation, because the element of trust in the judgment and discretion of an individual is entirely wanting. A corporation is without personality, and if it is selected as trustee or executor there can be no reliance upon individual discretions or even upon the continuance of the same administration. . . ."[94]

powers, and their power clearly includes power to appoint other agents.[99] And a Delaware court, apparently despairing of an intellectually satisfying reconciliation, decided simply to rest its decision on the observation that "while the maxim *delegatus non potest delegare* has been a principle of Anglo-Saxon law since the dim beginnings of modern times, it has lost its force as a result of the impact of big business and government."[100]

Regardless of the rationale, or lack of it, it is nevertheless true that the authorities are in complete agreement that the directors of modern business corporations have wide powers of delegation. Professor Ballantine succinctly summarized the view of most treatise writers in his classic work on corporations:

> "Directors are impliedly authorized to appoint officers and agents, and delegate to them power to act in the usual course of business of the corporation even in matters which involve the exercise of wide discretion. . . . [E]ven in the absence of express authority, an authority to delegate discretionary authority to committees, officers and agents must be implied from necessity and usage, for the directors cannot attend to all the current business operations of the corporation, and it is not customary for them to do so. . . ."[101]

The authorities seem also to be in agreement that "the trend of recent laws and decisions relating to the delegation of powers to transact the business affairs of corporations is toward a more liberal extension of such powers."[102]

Therefore, in concept, at least, regardless of whether the principles of trust law or those of corporate law are considered to be applicable, delegation of investment responsibility within the corporate structure should be permitted. However, relatively few authorities appear to have dealt specifically with the legal considerations involved in allocating investment responsibilities among the various strata of the corporate hierarchy of nonprofit institutions. The Second Restatement of Trusts, in distinguishing a charitable corporation from a charitable trust, makes the following observation:

> "It may be proper, for example, for the board [of a charitable corporation] to appoint a committee of its members to deal with the investment of the funds of the corporation, the board merely exercising a general supervision over the actions of the committee."[103]

The Model Non-Profit Corporation Act permits the board of directors of a nonprofit corporation to delegate most of its duties to committees composed of two or more directors (without, however, relieving the board of its ultimate responsibility), and provides further that the corporation may "elect or appoint officers and agents of the corporation . . . and define their duties."[104] Many states have adopted statutes which follow this general pattern,[105] and a few provide specifically for a finance committee to manage investments.[106] The Uniform Management of Institutional Funds Act provides for the delegation of investment responsibilities to committees, officers and employees of the institution.[107]*

We found only one case that could fairly be cited as authority against internal delegation. That was a rather confused decision rendered by the Supreme Judicial Court of Massachusetts in 1931.[108] The court had been asked for instructions as to the management of the Franklin Fund, which had been left by the will of Benjamin Franklin to the Town of Boston. For approximately a century the Fund was administered by a board of managers, which the legislature incorporated in 1908 under the name, The Franklin Foundation. In 1930, The Franklin Foundation voted to authorize the custodian of the Fund (the Treasurer of the City of Boston), "under the direction of the Treasurer of The Franklin Foundation," to invest part of the Fund in "securities in which funds of savings banks of this commonwealth may by law be invested."[109] The custodian asked the court for instructions as to whether he was free to use his own discretion in the investment of the Fund, or instead was bound by the directions of the Treasurer of the Foundation. Thus, the issue before the court was whether the administration of Mayor Curley of Boston, on the one hand, or the Foundation, on the other, was entitled to administer the Fund. The court held for the Foundation, but for some reason not apparent from the opinion it went out of its way to discuss delegation. It held that the direction to invest in securities in which savings banks could lawfully invest was too indefinite, "even when coupled with the bylaw of The Franklin Foundation to the effect that investments be made in such securities of that nature as the finance committee may direct."[110]** The opinion then went on to state the following:

---

*It provides also for external delegation. See p. 33, *infra*.
**The court ignored the apparent delegation to the Foundation's Treasurer; it mentioned only the reference in the bylaws to a finance committee.

"Every member [of The Franklin Foundation] is charged with the obligations of a trustee and must exercise as to every investment his best judgment and wise discretion. To make investments is fundamental, not merely administrative, in the administration of a trust. To be a manager of the fund involves the performance of personal duty, which as to investments to be made cannot be delegated to a committee or an agent. In general the duties of a trustee cannot be delegated. They are personal. Determination to make an investment does not necessarily require the affirmative vote of all members of the corporation but it requires action by a majority with opportunity and obligation, so far as reasonably practicable, for all to express their judgments. . . . The corporation does not supplant the individuals in the performance of these fundamental attributes of the trustees. As has been said, its purpose is to facilitate the administration and execution of the trust, not to relieve the individuals composing it from the obligations incident to their fiduciary obligation as managerial trustees. It follows that the city treasurer is bound to make new investments only upon specific direction manifested by a vote participated in by the individuals composing the corporation."[111]

The case can be distinguished from the normal case dealing with nonprofit corporations on two grounds. First, it seems clear that the court was confused as to the identity of the "trustee," and the identity of the trustee must of course be established before it can be determined whether he or it is improperly delegating investment decisions. At one point in the opinion, the court cited with approval its earlier holding in another case "that title [to the Fund] was in the municipality in trust for the purposes specified and not in the managers."[112] Yet in the paragraph quoted above, the individual members of the board of managers were referred to as the trustees. And later in the opinion, the court directed that certificates representing the investments of the Fund should specify the corporation as the trustee.[113]

Second, it should be noted that the Fund had been administered as a trust for a century before a special act of the legislature set up the corporation "to facilitate the administration and execution of the trust." In the circumstances, it is not surprising that trust principles were applied by the court, and there appears to be no reason to extend the holding to apply to charitable corporations in general.

In any event, despite the expansive sweep of the language, later decisions of the same court indicate clearly that it is not to be taken literally. A 1945 decision involved the administration of a trust by a corporate trustee.[114] The selection of securities had been delegated by the trustee to officers on its staff; they in turn reported once or twice a week to a "trust committee." The beneficiaries of the trust claimed that the arrangement constituted a breach of trust. The court dismissed their objections, pointing out that "Any corporation carrying on a trust business must of necessity act through officers or agents."[115]*

Two years later the same court was called upon to resolve a dispute relating to the administration of the funds of a charitable corporation.[117] The corporation had established a fund that was to receive all general donations to the corporation and use the income for the corporation's charitable purposes. For over half a century the fund was managed by trustees, who were not necessarily members of the corporate board. When the corporation attempted to transfer the assets in the fund to its general coffers, the trustees refused to turn them over, on the ground that they held the fund in trust. The corporation went to court, where it prevailed. The court observed that:

> "The legislature, in chartering the corporation, made it the sole custodian, manager, and almoner of its funds. . . . [W]e are of the opinion that . . . such trustees are not trustees at all in the legal sense but are mere officers and agents of the association and subject constantly to its control . . . ."[118]

Construed in that manner, the court found the delegation to be both regular and lawful.

Before the turn of the century the Supreme Court of Maine was faced with a factual situation somewhat similar to that of the *Curley* case. A sum had been bequeathed in trust to the City of Bangor for the promotion of education. The city established a board of five trustees to administer the trust. Eventually a dispute arose regarding the administration and the City Council sought to recover the bequeathed fund; the trustees refused to turn it over. The City Council prevailed, on the ground that the city itself is the trustee and the City Council speaks for the city. The court said that the Council could appoint agents to manage the fund, could discharge them and appoint others, or could dispense with them and manage the fund directly.[119]

---

*The court also pointed out that the corporate trustee accepted responsibility for the acts of its agents, and did not try to shield itself from claims of the trust beneficiaries on the ground that it lacked such responsibility.[116] That is an issue not presented by the delegation of investment responsibility by a charitable corporation, which is itself the beneficiary of its funds.

Similarly, a Pennsylvania case involved the administration of a gift that had been made in trust to the City of Philadelphia. The donor had provided that it was to be administered by the commissioners of a certain park. The court found the following arrangement for managing investments to be "most satisfactory":

> "The purchase and sale of all securities is supervised by a special committee, of which [the treasurer of the commission, a highly regarded financial expert] is a member. The committee keeps full minutes of its deliberations and reviews the trust portfolio at frequent intervals. Experts in various branches of the investment business are invited to sit with the committee. Between meetings the list of investments held by the estate is submitted to various investment bankers, for review and suggestions. All of the securities are presently held by the Philadelphia National Bank, as custodian."[120]

It is not clear whether the committee was composed of commissioners, but it was clearly something less than the full commission.*

Finally, although it used trust law as a guide, an Arkansas court raised no issue of delegation in approving an investment made by members of a college finance committee.[122] It does not appear from the opinion where the committee stood in the hierarchy of the college administration.

The foregoing cases support the conclusion that directors of nonprofit corporations can lawfully delegate investment responsibility to committees or responsible individuals within the institution. But directors may decide that the institution's needs can best be served by an outside investment manager. We discuss that problem in the following section.

(C) EXTERNAL DELEGATION

(i) *Statutes.* There are a few statutes that deal with the right of a nonprofit corporation to delegate investment responsibilities to an investment manager outside the corporate structure. The Uniform Management of Institutional Funds Act is the broadest of these, providing for such delegation to "independent investment advisors, investment counsel or managers, banks, or trust companies."[123]

---

*The court also noted that the trustee is the city and not the commission or the individual commissioners. For that reason no accountings were required upon a change in personnel of the commissioners. The court observed that this was equally true in respect of the officers and directors of eleemosynary institutions.[121]

New York and Pennsylvania both permit nonprofit corporations to transfer endowment funds to a corporate trustee, which is defined as a bank and trust company or a trust company incorporated under the laws of the state, or a national banking association having fiduciary powers and having its principal office in the state. The board of directors of the nonprofit corporation is specifically relieved of all liability for the administration of the funds as long as they are being administered by the corporate trustee.[124]

California has a similar statute, which permits delegation in whole or in part to one or more trust companies or banks authorized to conduct business within the state.[125] Although the directors of the delegating corporation are not specifically relieved of responsibility for the administration of the delegated funds during the period of delegation, it seems fair to assume that was the intention of the legislature.

A Louisiana statute provides that any educational institution within the state may, if it wishes, deposit its funds with the state treasury, for investment in bonds or obligations of Louisiana or the United States to be selected by the Auditor of Public Accounts or the State Treasurer.[126]

(ii) *Other direct authorities.* Very few rulings can be found that deal directly with the power of a nonprofit corporation to delegate investment responsibility to an external manager in the absence of a controlling statute.

A Connecticut court refused to remove trustees of a school or hold them liable for losses resulting from the mismanagement of funds that they had turned over to a lawyer and real estate agent of good reputation for investment.[127] On the other hand, the Attorney General of Massachusetts rendered an opinion four decades ago to the effect that the trustees of the Bradford Durfee School could not delegate investment responsibilities to the Durfee Trust Company.[128] The manner and extent of the attempted delegation are not clearly specified in the opinion.

The most helpful case found involved a bequest of property in trust to individual trustees to establish a museum in Massachusetts. Pursuant to court order they established a corporation to administer the property. The corporation entered into an agency agreement with a bank, pursuant to which the bank was to act as custodian of the corporation's securities, advise it as to investments, and handle its bookkeeping. Some time later the Attorney General sued to remove the trustees. He prevailed in the trial court, but the Supreme Judicial Court reversed on appeal, saying:

> "The judge found numerous irregularities in the agency agreement entered into between the trustees and the bank. He concluded, among other things, that the trustees improperly delegated their duties as trustees to the bank. We do not agree. None of the trustees had much, if any, experience in the field of investments, and it was entirely proper for them to seek expert advice. The record reveals that the trustees were consulted on the investments made and gave their approval to such investments. Although the will provided that the trustees were to receive reasonable compensation for their services, they served without compensation. Thus, the fees paid to the bank under the agency agreement did not place any undue burden on the trust. Boston v. Curley, 276 Mass. 549, 562, 177 N.E. 557. While a trustee cannot surrender to another his duties with respect to investments, he may seek the advice of those better qualified. That is what was done here. . . ."[129]

A number of cases were found that dealt with attempts by one charitable corporation to transfer all or substantially all of its assets to another charitable corporation. As a practical matter, such a total abandonment of legal interest has little in common with the limited delegation of investment responsibility with which we are concerned, but the issue involved could be considered one of delegation in a broad sense and for that reason we discuss the cases here.

In Delaware, a charitable corporation had transferred over half its endowment to a new charitable foundation. One of the members of the first corporation attacked the transfer, arguing that "an incorporated charitable foundation is governed by the same rules of law as are trustees of a charitable trust," and that the transfer would constitute "a delegation [which] is an abrogation of the trust upon which they hold such funds as trustees."[130] The court held, however, that no technical trust is created by an outright gift to a charitable corporation, but at most a trust in the loose sense of the word, the extent and measure of which are to be determined by the charter and bylaws of the corporation. The court then concluded:

> "This being so, a charitable trust in the technical sense is not created and the test as to the legality of action taken by the governing board of the corporation is to be determined in accordance with principles of corporate law rather than principles

governing the fiduciary relationship between trustees of a technical trust and their trust."[131]

The plaintiff pointed to the magnitude of the transfer, but the court said that this was merely a matter of degree, to be left to the judgment of the directors "under familiar principles of corporate law."[132] The transfer was upheld.

An Arkansas court, citing corporate law, upheld a similar transfer on the ground that it had been ratified by the inaction of the members of the transferor charitable corporation, "whose relation to that organization is not dissimilar to that of shareholders in the ordinary private corporation."[133]

A similar transfer was approved as a proper exercise of corporate power by a Kentucky court, which observed that the very nature of an educational institution demands adaptability and flexibility in administration:

> "It contemplated, by every reasonable implication, that new methods, new people, even new ideas, would be employed, when approved by the governing body of the institution. . . . For the past to bind it to unchangeableness would be to prevent growth, applying the treatment to the head that the Chinese do to the feet."[134]*

(iii) *Analogies: trust law.* Faced with a dearth of authorities dealing directly with the power of a nonprofit corporation to delegate investment responsibility to an external manager, we turn for purposes of analogy to a discussion of the law governing the right of trustees to delegate such responsibility. As the first step in that discussion, consider the nature of a trust.

Trustees are typically chosen as such because the settlor of the trust places special confidence in their judgment and ability. If trustees are allowed casually to surrender the administration of the trust to strangers, there seems little point in having designated the trustees to act in the first place; indeed, the reason for establishing the trust itself may have been lost. It has therefore become an established precept of trust law that the trustee must attend personally to the most important aspects

---

*Most of the cases dealing with the transfer of assets of one charitable corporation to another appear to have followed the cases quoted in text in applying the principles of corporate law to the solution of the problem.[135] A few have considered the matter to be one of contract law.[136] Others have applied the doctrines of *cy pres* and deviation.[137]

of administering the trust. The reasoning of the Supreme Court of the United States in a decision handed down a century ago is typical:

> "Letters of administration are a trust. They are granted . . . because of confidence reposed in the grantee. They require him to take exclusive charge of the personal property of his intestate and to bring to its administration his own personal attention and judgment. He has no right to allow others to control it or to share in its administration. If he does, he exposes it to unnecessary hazards and subjects it to the disposition of persons in whom the officer of the law has reposed no confidence. . . ."[138]

Although *some* duties of a trustee may properly be discharged through an agent, the very essence of the typical trust is the investment of trust funds for the benefit of the beneficiaries of the trust. Therefore, the authorities are in agreement, at least in the abstract, that "the choice and supervision of investments . . . are absolutely non-delegable."[139]

We shall examine in some detail the cases dealing with delegation by trustees, but two points should be noted at the outset.

The first point is that the rationale of the trust rule prohibiting delegation of investment decisions has very little application to the typical charitable corporation dealing with its endowment funds. The Supreme Court of New Hampshire, in a recent decision upholding the constitutionality of the Uniform Management of Institutional Funds Act, made the point as follows:

> "The proposed Act applies exclusively to funds held by an eleemosynary institution for its exclusive use, benefit or purposes. Hence there exists no conflict of interest between an income beneficiary and a remainderman, nor is there the usual fiduciary relationship toward beneficiaries which exists when a trust fund is not held for the exclusive use, benefit or purposes of its administrator as are the funds to be regulated by this Act. These institutions are in a situation with regard to their endowment funds similar to that of directors of a business corporation with respect to the administration of its property. . . ."[140]

It will be remembered that the Second Restatement of Trusts states that the trustee is under a duty *to the beneficiary* not to delegate the doing of certain acts. A charitable corporation is itself the beneficiary of the funds it administers. It receives its funds not because of its special expertise in investing, but because the donors want it to have the benefit of the funds.

37

The second point to be noted about the rule prohibiting trustees from delegating investment decisions is that it has been the subject of increasing criticism and, perhaps as a result, it is no longer nearly as absolute as some authorities would have one believe. The criticism is exemplified by an article that pointed out that "[t]his restringent rule makes efficient trust administration very difficult,"[141] and complained that:

> "From one side of his mouth the chancellor admonishes the trustee to manage the trust property as a prudent man would his own; from the other side he warns him and all who deal with him that the law in its wisdom will not permit prudent management according to twentieth century standards."[142]

England, the wellspring of trust law, enacted a statute half a century ago which substantially abolished the rule against delegation by trustees:

> "Trustees or personal representatives may, instead of acting personally, employ and pay an agent, whether a solicitor, banker, stockbroker, or other person to transact any business or do any act required to be transacted or done in the execution of the trust, or the administration of the testator's or the intestate's estate, including the receipt and payment of money, and shall be entitled to be allowed and paid all charges and expenses so incurred, and shall not be responsible for the default of any such agent if employed in good faith."[143]

A number of the Commonwealth countries have followed suit.[144] And in this country the rule has been steadily eroded. For example, a century ago a trustee in New York could not invest in corporate stock, because such an investment was considered to be an improper delegation of the trustee's control; it would be difficult to find a knowledgeable person today who would think of such an investment as a "delegation."[145] Four decades ago the same argument was used to prevent trustees from investing in management-type investment companies, an investment now considered to be proper almost everywhere.[146]

Although we perceive no cogent rationale for applying trust principles in determining the extent of a nonprofit corporation's power to delegate, it should be noted (as we observed above) that those principles do allow a trustee to discharge *some* of his duties through an agent. The dividing line between acts that can be delegated by a trustee and

38

those that cannot is not always easy to draw. Many authorities define the dichotomy in terms of discretionary acts, on the one hand, and purely ministerial acts, on the other. For example, the Second Restatement of Agency provides that:

> "Unless otherwise agreed, an agent cannot properly delegate to another *the exercise of discretion* in the use of a power held for the benefit of the principal."[147] (Emphasis supplied.)

But it seems self-evident that even the most menial of tasks involves *some* discretion, and the true relevance of discretion is therefore not its presence or absence but its degree.[148] The Second Restatement of Trusts therefore formulates the rule without direct reference to discretion:

> "The trustee is under a duty to the beneficiary not to delegate to others the doing of *acts which the trustee can reasonably be required personally to perform.*"[149] (Emphasis supplied.)

Discretion is only one of the factors which the Restatement considers to be relevant in applying that rule:

> "In considering what acts a trustee can properly delegate the following circumstances, among others, may be of importance: (1) the amount of discretion involved; (2) the value and character of the property involved; (3) whether the property is principal or income; (4) the proximity or remoteness of the subject matter of the trust; (5) the character of the act as one involving professional skill or facilities possessed or not possessed by the trustee himself."[150]*

In determining whether it is reasonable to expect a trustee personally to perform a given act, courts tend to look to the hypothetical prudent man. As Professor Bogert observed:

> "If the hypothetical business man, in view of the character of the act and his own qualifications for doing it, would take direct personal control of the function, then the courts expect the trustee to do likewise; but, if the business man would employ an outside

---

*If the agent has skills or training not possessed by the trustee himself, delegation is more likely to be condoned.[151] Thus, it was held to be reasonable for an executor to allow an attorney to handle the sale of real estate that constituted part of the estate and to collect the proceeds at closing. The executor escaped liability when the attorney embezzled the proceeds.[152]

expert, or use a regularly employed agent or servant, then the trustee is given similar liberty."[153]

The best statement of this approach that we found was that of an English judge speaking in the last century:

> "It seems to me that on general principles a trustee ought to conduct the business of the trust in the same manner that an ordinary prudent man of business would conduct his own, and that beyond that there is no liability or obligation on the trustee. In other words, a trustee is not bound because he is a trustee to conduct business in other than the ordinary and usual way in which similar business is conducted by mankind in transactions of their own. It never could be reasonable to make a trustee adopt further and better precautions than an ordinary prudent man of business would adopt, or to conduct the business in any other way. If it were otherwise, no one would be a trustee at all. He is not paid for it. He says, 'I take all reasonable precautions and all the precautions which are deemed reasonable by prudent men of business, and beyond that I am not required to go.' "[154]

Following this reasoning, a number of courts have upheld the delegation of investment decisions by trustees when the situation warranted such delegation. For example, the executor of a New Hampshire estate employed attorneys in Wisconsin to inspect Wisconsin lands to which the estate had a claim, to value them, and to select those which in the attorneys' opinion were worth redeeming from persons who had purchased them for taxes. The executor sent to the attorneys funds from the estate to be used for this purpose, and the attorneys misappropriated them. Recognizing that the attorneys were not only on the scene but were familiar with Wisconsin real property values, which the executor was not, the court refused to hold the executor liable for the delegation:

> "The general rule of law, that an executor cannot delegate his office to others, is unquestioned, but like most legal principles it is bounded and defined by reason. . . . If it is reasonably necessary for a trustee to employ agents or attorneys, and if he uses ordinary care in their selection, and a proper supervision over the business entrusted to them, he cannot be held liable for their indiscretion resulting without fault on his part. . . ."[155]

In an Ohio case it was claimed to be an unlawful delegation of authority for a trustee to hire a professional management company to manage an office building that constituted the principal asset of the trust. The court noted that the building was 26 years old and was beginning to experience a struggle for its economic existence against larger, more modern buildings. Applying the test of the prudent man handling his own affairs, it held that the delegation was proper.[156]

The most informative trust decision found happened to employ the most colorful language. A fund had been left in trust to county judges in Missouri and their successors in office for the purpose of providing scholarships. The judges turned the fund over to successive county treasurers, one of whom (after the practice had continued for some decades) became insolvent and lost part of the fund. The judges then in office were held liable for the loss by a trial court, but on appeal the judgment was reversed. The appellate court noted the general rule that trustees must retain custody of trust funds and execute the trust themselves, and went on to observe:

> "But there are exceptions to the rule, arising from necessity, or from the common custom of mankind, in which the trustee is entitled to employ an agent and will not be liable for losses occurring from the act of the agent, if the selection was a proper one. . . . Many illustrations could be added, e.g. where the trust consists of a large number of houses, where the rents are small and payable monthly; the trustee could attend to the business himself; but it is not usual for owners to do so themselves and trustees are not expected to. Or if the trust consists of a cattle ranch, the trustees could feed and herd the cattle themselves, but it would be unreasonable to expect it. . . .
>
> ". . . .
>
> "In this case the defendants might have kept the securities and cash in a strong box in a bank or safe deposit, with triplicate keys, one held by each, and all necessary to open the box. But this is not the common custom of mankind. They might have made all the loans and collections themselves, going in solemn form, in single file or in solid phalanx after the delinquent debtors, and returning, laden with spoils, have proceeded in a body to lay the treasures away in the triply guarded depository, but this is not the custom of trustees. In short they might have constituted themselves a constant guard of honor over the fund, like the dragon guarding the Golden Fleece at Colchis, to prevent some Jason from running away with it, but their eccentricity in so doing would have excited wonderment in our practical day and generation. But they were not obliged to do any of these ostentatious acts. They were *judges,* not mere private trustees selected on

> account of special confidence of the creator of the trust. . . .
> They were trustees because they were judges not judges because
> they were trustees and not because they were selected with special
> confidence in their fitness to administer this trust. They had a right
> to employ an agent. . . ."[157]

To summarize, it is unquestionably a rule of general application that
trustees are not permitted to delegate to others the making of investment
decisions for the trust. But the rationale of that rule simply does not
apply to the endowment funds of charitable corporations. Such corporations are not chosen as "trustees" because of any special confidence in
their ability to make investment decisions; like the county judges in
Missouri,* their role as "trustees" is quite incidental to their primary
reason for existence. With that factor removed from consideration, the
trust principles discussed above would seem to us to sanction the
delegation of investment decisions by charitable corporations. It would
seem patently unreasonable, for example, for the law to require the
unpaid, part-time directors of the typical educational institution personally to make buy-sell decisions for a multimillion-dollar endowment,
when there are skilled personnel available to make the decisions more
efficiently and at greater profit for the institution. It would seem equally
unreasonable for the law to overrule the judgment of the directors if
after conscientious search they decide that the investment manager best
qualified to make such decisions for their particular institution is a
professional operating outside their corporate structure, rather than an
employee of the institution. And in the words of the New Hampshire
decision discussed above,** trust principles, like most legal principles,
are "bounded and defined by reason."

(iv) *Analogies: corporate law*. As we have seen, even if a nonprofit
corporation were viewed technically as a trustee, trust law should allow
use of an outside investment manager. However, the better approach, as
we suggested above, would apply the law of corporations, not of trusts;
and corporate law is quite liberal in allowing delegation.

A few examples of external delegation by business corporations should
suffice for purposes of analogy in determining the extent to which investment responsibilities can be delegated by nonprofit corporations. Perhaps
the most striking example is afforded by investment companies, or mutual

---

*See p. 41, *supra*.

**See p. 40, *supra*.

42

funds, which traditionally have been managed by outside investment advisers pursuant to a contract.* Virtually the entire management of most mutual funds is entrusted to such an adviser, an arrangement explicitly recognized by the Investment Company Act of 1940.[158]**

Public utilities also sometimes contract with managers outside their corporate structures for the performance of wide-ranging managing functions.[160] And management contracts are frequently used by smaller corporations "which are thereby able to secure the part-time services of experts more competent than corporate directors or officers but whose full-time services the corporation could not afford."[161]

A case similar to the last-mentioned category arose half a century ago in California. A group of iron and steel manufacturers had established a joint committee that was granted full and exclusive powers for three years to represent all members of the group in collective bargaining with employees of the members. The defendants failed to make agreed payments to the group, and when sued by the other members, the defendants defended on the ground, *inter alia,* that the establishment of the joint committee constituted an improper delegation of corporate authority. The court held the delegation to be proper, saying:

> "The modern method of transacting corporate business requires that agents frequently, in cases where action by the board of directors would be impracticable or unfeasible, represent the corporation in dealings requiring the exercise of a great degree of discretion. . . . The power delegated [in the case at bar] was merely the full authority to handle a branch of the corporations' affairs, i.e., the regulation of the conditions of employment. . . ."[162]***

---

*The practice had its origins in the early funds organized by lawyer trustees who could not afford to spend the time required to manage the accounts of small clients and therefore pooled them, in order to give them jointly the benefit of the trustees' experience. The closest analogy in the field of endowment funds is The Common Fund for Nonprofit Organizations. See pp. 12-13, *supra.*

**The Act assumes an external investment adviser and provides protection against abuse of the practice. The contract with the investment adviser must be in writing, must be approved by a majority of the outstanding securities of the investment company, and must provide for termination by the investment company at any time, without penalty, upon not more than 60 days' written notice. If it is to continue in effect for more than two years, it must be approved at least annually by the board of directors or by vote of a majority of the outstanding voting securities of the investment company. If the contract is assigned, it is to be automatically terminated.[159]

***A similar case arose even earlier in New York, where a trade association was given power to regulate and control labor relations for its members. When the association attempted to decree a union shop, the court struck the action down as against public policy, but made it clear that it had no objection to the basic arrangement.[163]

43

A hotel corporation in New York entered into a management contract with a management company owned or controlled by the majority stockholder of the hotel corporation. A minority stockholder of the hotel corporation sued to have the contract declared illegal and void, but the court held against him on the following reasoning:

> "Whether the hotel could better be operated through the medium of a management company presented a question of business judgment. If the decision had been arrived at as a result of an honest, prudent and careful belief of the directors that it was for the best interest of the hotel company, then that determination would not be subject to interference by the courts, even though an error in judgment may have been committed. . . ."[164]

Similarly, a court in Pennsylvania had no difficulty in upholding an extremely broad delegation of managerial responsibilities by a failing corporation, since the board of directors (which was composed, the court observed, of "high grade and well known business men") remained in existence and passed upon issues involving broad company policy.[165]

A Delaware case, which involved internal rather than external delegation, is nevertheless of interest because of the court's approach to the problem. A stockholder's derivative suit sought to hold the directors of United States Steel liable for alleged damages suffered by the corporation as a result of an agreement by corporate officers to have the corporation pay sums to local governments in lieu of taxes. The aggregate amount thus paid, which the plaintiff claimed was "not required or permitted by . . . law," amounted to $29,000,000. Approval of the payment was not sought from the board of directors; indeed, there was no evidence that the board was even aware of it. In granting the defendants' motion for summary judgment, the court stated:

> "In short I am persuaded that the magnitude of Steel's operations requires substantial delegation. And that is as permissible in law as it is necessary in fact. . . . I cannot say that the broad managerial delegation adopted by Steel as a business judgment is wrong as a matter of law because it permitted management to do what was done here."[166]

But there are limits to the right of business directors to delegate managerial responsibilities, and for our purposes those limits are particularly instructive. If the courts do permit the delegation of investment responsibilities by charitable corporations, as we believe they will, it seems likely that the limitations imposed by the courts on delegation by business corporations will constitute the touchstone for delineating similar limitations for charitable corporations. In the words of a Minnesota court:

> "The trustees of a charitable corporation, as members of its managing body, are charged with the same fidelity in the performance of functional duty as the directors of a private business corporation. . . . The law confines the business management of a corporation to its directors and they are vested with a fiduciary responsibility to administer its affairs. . . . Directors may not agree . . . to abstain from discharging their fiduciary duty to participate actively and fully in the management of corporate affairs."[167]

As that holding indicates, the principal lesson to be learned in this connection from the law of business corporations is that while directors may *delegate* responsibilities, they may not *abdicate* responsibilities.[168] Or, as a California court aptly put it:

> "The board may grant authority to act, but it cannot delegate its function to govern. . . ."[169]

From that lesson all secondary lessons follow. Thus, delegation is more likely to be upheld if it is terminable at will or after a relatively short period of time.[170] A delegation of specific, relatively narrow duties is safer than a delegation of all or most of the board's functions.[171] And the courts are less likely to interfere if the board retains ultimate power to direct or reverse the delegate's action, rather than ceding exclusive power to the delegate.[172]*

(v) *Ratification.* The subject of ratification is important enough to warrant separate discussion, because for those directors of charitable corporations who prefer not to take the lead in making investment decisions, it provides an alternative method for the discharge of fiduciary duties. Whether one looks to trust principles or to the tenets of corporate law, all that the law requires is that a fiduciary devote to the matter at hand that degree of personal care and attention required by the

---

*Similar reasoning can be found in cases that construe agreements by a corporation to hire specified persons as officers or managers. If it is argued that such an agreement prevents the directors from discharging the individual for lack of fidelity, the agreement is normally struck down as against public policy.[173]

circumstances. If the action of a delegate can be reversed without significant cost, a prompt and careful review by the fiduciary of the delegate's action should serve the purposes of the fiduciary account—and the requirements of the law—fully as well as if the fiduciary personally took the action.

Therefore, Fletcher merely sets forth the black-letter law of corporations when he says:

> "When a contract is made or other act done for a corporation by a person acting without authority, the directors may ratify his act and render it binding, if it is an act which they could have authorized. This involves no delegation of their powers. . . ."[174]

And, as Professor Scott points out, the same thing is equally true under the law of trusts.[175]

A famous Pennsylvania decision of a century ago is particularly instructive, because it indicates not only the factors considered by the court in determining that a particular delegation of investment responsibility by a trustee was excessive, but also discusses the role of ratification. Acting under a power of attorney from a co-trustee, a trustee had effected a transfer of shares of stock owned by the trust and had absconded with the proceeds. In holding the defendants liable for permitting the transfer to be made, the court said:

> "[The power of attorney] was a general power to sell stocks, embracing everything in the estate . . . and it was without any limit as to price, or reference as to the time, place and manner of sale. Nor did the principal reserve any veto or check upon the act of his agent. The latter was to exercise all the discretion which by law vested in the former. Whether the price was sufficient, or the sale itself, at the particular time, and in the then condition of the stock market was judicious, were questions which the agent was empowered to decide without any consultation with his principal. In this respect we think the power of attorney was invalid. If after making the sale the attorney had reported the same to his principal, and the latter had ratified it, *thus exercising his discretion,* I have no doubt the transfer under the power would have been good, and herein the defendants were remiss. With such a general power delegating discretion, they should have required some evidence of the ratification of the sale by the principal...."[176]

In another Pennsylvania case involving a claim of unlawful delegation, an executrix had executed an "agency account" with a bank, whereby

46

the bank "became the agent and attorney-in-fact for the executrix, formally received all securities, agreed to collect the income, make such investments as she should authorize and 'to suggest suitable investments for any principal moneys in hand. . . .' "[177] The terms of the instrument did not disclose any delegation of investment discretion, but the court nevertheless looked beyond the instrument to the actual conduct of the parties. Although it found that the bank had exceeded the bounds of purely ministerial duties, the court did not find an "improper delegation of discretionary duties for the breach of which the executrix could be surcharged for loss," for the following reasons:

> "Here the executrix maintained constant contact with her agent; she had numerous conversations with [a vice-president of the bank]; and she knew of all transactions and approved them. . . . What Scott on Trusts (p. 916) says with regard to the delegation of duties in *Bohlen's Estate* . . . is applicable here: 'It was the duty of the [executrix] to exercise [her] own discretion in determining whether the securities should be sold and at what price. The result would be different if [the executrix] had exercised [her] discretion in determining to sell the specific securities and in fixing the price, *or if the sale had been reported to [her] and in the exercise of [her] discretion [she] had ratified it.*' "[178] (Italics in original.)

An executor of an estate attempted in an old New York case to defend against a suit for specific performance of a contract to sell the estate's land, on the ground that the contract had been entered into on his behalf by an unauthorized agent. The court found that the executor had ratified the contract and therefore held for the plaintiff, saying:

> "Assuming that [the agent], in this case, acted without authority from the defendant, the latter had a right, when the contract came to his knowledge, either to repudiate or to confirm it. In determining upon one or the other course, he brought into exercise those personal qualifications on account of which he is presumed to have been selected by the testator. The law does not allow him to commit the power with which he is entrusted to another, for perhaps that other would bind the estate to a transaction which the former might not have considered advantageous and safe if he had acted directly upon it. The reason fails where the person actually entrusted with the authority has, with a full knowledge of the facts, ratified the act of one who has assumed to act as his agent."[179]

A number of other cases to the same effect may be cited.[180] But it should be emphasized that they do not suggest that a fiduciary can discharge his duty by perfunctorily rubber-stamping the actions of his agent.[181] It is assumed that the fiduciary carefully reviews the action of the agent before making the decision to ratify it. The point is that the cases make it clear that while a fiduciary must exercise his own discretion, he may do so by ratifying the act of an agent as well as by acting himself.

(D) SUMMARY AND RECOMMENDATIONS

The directors of virtually all charitable corporations do in fact delegate investment decisions, either to a committee or an officer or an agent. Our survey and the Harris Survey both found that investment decisions for half of the institutions of higher learning in America are being made by investment managers outside the corporate structure. Is such widespread delegation legal?

Delegation within the corporate structure should present no problem, provided that the directors take reasonable steps to keep abreast of investment decisions made for their endowment funds and in fact discharge their duty of supervision. In states in which the Uniform Management of Institutional Funds Act has been adopted, delegation to an outside investment manager is specifically authorized. And even in the absence of statutory sanction in the remaining jurisdictions, we believe that the courts should and will uphold the delegation of investment decisions to an external investment manager, assuming once again that the directors continue to exercise overall supervision.

Our conclusion remains the same regardless of whether trust principles or principles of corporate law are applied. It is unquestionably true that trustees are not normally permitted to delegate to others the making of investment decisions for the trust. But the rationale for that rule is based upon the emphasis placed by the typical grantor on the investment expertise of his chosen trustee. By contrast, the typical donor of a charitable gift focuses upon the welfare and purposes of the recipient institution, not upon its investment skill. With the factor of investment expertise removed from the picture, the trust principles discussed above seem to us to sanction the delegation of investment decisions by charitable corporations. Certainly such delegation is sanctioned by corporate law.

Regardless of whether the delegate is within or without the corporate structure, the courts will be more likely to uphold delegation if the directors can demonstrate that they have taken appropriate steps to monitor and supervise the investment process. Written goals and guidelines for the investment of the institution's endowment funds should be drafted by the board, working in conjunction with the investment manager, and the board should make certain that it receives reports on a sufficiently current basis to assure itself that the guidelines are being followed and the goals met. When it has so assured itself, good practice would call for formal ratification of the action of the delegate.

In establishing goals, the board will want to consider the role that revenue from endowment funds is expected to play in the finances of the particular institution. For example, a choice should be made between investing for total return and investing for current yield. The board will also have to balance the degree of risk it seems appropriate to run in the investment of the fund against the return expected from the investment. The board and the investment manager should be in agreement on the approximate balance to be struck between equity and debt securities in the portfolio, and that balance should be reexamined from time to time in light of changes in the economy.

Depending upon the circumstances, it may be appropriate for the board and the investment manager to agree in advance on percentage or dollar limitations for investments in any one industry or company. The board may wish to instruct the manager to avoid investments in particular companies or industries, or in unlisted securities, restricted securities or foreign securities. It would be wise specifically to prohibit investments that would violate the provisions of Treasury Regulations § 53.4944-1(a)(2), dealing with "jeopardizing investments."* It might also be appropriate for the board in some instances to give advance approval to lists of securities from which the investment manager is authorized to make purchases or sales for the endowment fund.

While consideration should be given to matters such as the foregoing, we do not mean to suggest that all of them or even most of them should be incorporated in every set of guidelines. The board should not attempt to fabricate a straightjacket for itself and its investment manager. The

---

*No category of investments is treated as a *per se* violation of the regulations, but the regulations list certain investments "which will be closely scrutinized." These include trading in securities on margin, trading in commodity futures, investments in working interests in oil and gas wells, the purchase of "puts" and "calls" and "straddles," the purchase of warrants, and selling short.

guidelines should be concerned with matters of broad policy, not detailed minutia. The goal should be for the board and manager, working together, to develop guidelines within which the manager can function with the desired flexibility, but that will assure that the investment program followed is one designed to serve the long-range interests of the particular institution.

The selection of the investment manager should receive the most careful attention; his reputation and record should of course be checked.* Whether or not it exercises the right to deal with the portfolio directly, the board should avoid any contractual arrangement that would prevent it from doing so. It should have the power to direct a specific purchase or sale, or to reverse actions of the investment manager. The manager should be subject to discharge at any time at the will of the board, upon notice of not more than 60 days.

Again, the essential point is that the board must exercise responsible supervision over the investment of the institution's funds, as it does over all of the institution's other affairs. If the courts are satisfied that this has been done, they should find no fault with the delegation to skilled agents of the power to make specific investment decisions.

Conclusion

The financial problems of America's nonprofit institutions grow more grave with each passing year. Endowments contribute a steadily decreasing proportion of the income needed to keep those institutions in operation, not because endowments have not grown, but because the demands for income have increased voraciously. It is vitally important that endowments be managed with an expertise and skill sufficient to raise their productivity to the highest attainable level.

There are those who have claimed that the law inhibits the efficient management of endowment funds, that it fetters and shackles those who would do a better job if they were free to do so. It has been the

---

*The Ford Foundation's Advisory Committee on Endowment Management suggested that in choosing an investment manager, a prospective client should inquire as to the "number, type and size of accounts handled [by the manager]; degree of homogeneity in their objectives; how many were lost in recent years and why; degree to which they are discretionary; aggregate funds under management; number and kinds of personnel; background and length of service of key people; degree to which their time goes into non-portfolio activities (e.g. administration and marketing); personnel turn-over and reasons therefor; policies for attracting and keeping outstanding people; who makes the portfolio decisions and how; research available and how it reaches the portfolio manager; changes in key strategies and methods of operation during the last few years; special strengths and weaknesses of the organization."[182]

purpose of this report and its predecessor to examine the validity of that claim.

The claim is engendered and nurtured by a fundamental misconception of the role of law in our society. Law is the lubricant that enables our system to work. It must be flexible, adapting to the changing needs of changing times. Our courts cannot and do not march to the cadence of ancient learning, blindly applying to the problem at hand principles derived from totally different circumstances. They look instead to the best teaching of the past as a guide to the intelligent solution of the problems of today. Our nonprofit institutions have nothing to fear from such an approach to their problems.

Notes

1. *See, e.g.,* Adams, *The Cost of Higher Education, 1971-72,* 7 COLLEGE MANAGE-
   MENT 10 (1972); Cheit, *The Economic Squeeze in Education is Pervasive,* N.Y. Times,
   Jan. 10, 1972, § E (annual education review), at 2; CHEIT, THE NEW DEPRESSION
   IN HIGHER EDUCATION (1971); Corson, *Reversing the Process,* 11 COLLEGE +
   U.J., Mar. 1972, at 4; Crimmins, *Our Friends in Nonprofitland Say a Major Financial
   Crisis is on the Way,* VI INSTITUTIONAL INVESTOR, Aug. 1972, at 34; Geiger, *The
   Impending Crisis of the Liberal Arts Colleges,* 57 AAUPB 500 (1971); JELLEMA,
   REDDER AND MUCH REDDER (1971); CARNEGIE COMMISSION ON HIGHER
   EDUCATION, THE MORE EFFECTIVE USE OF RESOURCES, vii, 2-3 (1972);
   Editorial, *A Great Depression,* 48 PEABODY J. ED. 158 (1971); Editorial, *Universities
   in Jeopardy,* N.Y. Times, Dec. 21, 1971, at 36; Frank, *Colleges Need Funds,* N.Y. Times,
   Jan. 6, 1972, at 36 (letter to editor).
2. *Fenn College v. Nance,* 4 Ohio Misc. 183, 190, 210 N.E.2d 418, 422 (C.P. Cuyahoga
   County 1965).
3. LOUIS HARRIS & ASSOCIATES, INC., MANAGING ENDOWMENT FUNDS: A
   SURVEY OF ENDOWED INSTITUTIONS 8 (1971).
4. *Id.* at 28.
5. MECKLING & JENSEN, UNIVERSITY ENDOWMENTS AND SPENDING POLI-
   CIES 11-13 (unpublished report, University of Rochester, 1970); MALKIEL & MES-
   TRES, THE DEFINITION OF ENDOWMENT INCOME 8-12 (unpublished report,
   Princeton University, 1970); ADVISORY COMMITTEE ON ENDOWMENT MAN-
   AGEMENT, MANAGING EDUCATIONAL ENDOWMENTS 19-21 (2d ed. 1972).
6. Baldwin, *Conventional Principal and Income Accounting and its Effect on Institutional
   Investment Policy,* 25 FINANCIAL ANAL. J. Mar.-Apr. 1969, at 60, 64; *see* ADVISORY
   COMMITTEE, *supra* note 5, at 9 and 17.
7. David, *Principal and Income—Obsolete Concepts,* 23 PA. B.Q. 247, 247-48 (1972).
8. Breen, *Legal Aspects of Substituting Common Stocks for Fixed Income Securities Under
   the Prudent Man Rule,* 159 N.Y.L.J. 4, col. 1 (June 27, 1968).
9. *Id.* at col. 3; Comment, *Prudent Man Investment of Trust Funds during Inflation,* 39
   Calif. L. Rev. 380, 387-88 (1951); Comment, *Investment Duties of Trustees and the
   Problem of Unduly Conservative Trust Investments,* 61 Mich. L. Rev. 1545, 1557-60
   (1963).
10. *Report of the Treasurer of Yale University, 1966-67,* 5 (Jan. 27, 1968).
11. David, *supra* note 7, at 251.
12. Baldwin, *supra* note 6, at 67.
13. LOUIS HARRIS, *supra* note 3.
14. *Id.* at 28, 35.
15. *Ibid.*
16. *Id.* at 34.
17. NACUBO, COMMENTS ON AUDIT GUIDE DRAFT FORWARDED TO AICPA 2
    (Special Report 72-13, Dec. 18, 1972).
18. CAL. CORP. CODE § 10251 (West 1972); MASS. GEN. LAWS ANN. ch. 68, § 32
    (1972); N.H. REV. STAT. ANN. § 421:2 (1971).
19. UNIFORM MANAGEMENT OF INSTITUTIONAL FUNDS ACT §§ 2 and 6.
20. *Id.* at § 3.
21. CAL. CIV. CODE §§ 2290.1 through 2290.12 (1973).
22. *Opinion of the Justices,* 306 A.2d 55 (N.H. 1973).
23. *In re Gardner's Trust,* 266 Minn. 127, 123 N.W.2d 69 (1963); *In re Arens,* 41 N.J. 364,
    197 A.2d 1 (1963); *Catherwood Trust,* 405 Pa. 61, 173 A.2d 86 (1961), *overruling
    Crawford Est.,* 362 Pa. 458, 67 A.2d 124 (1949). *But cf. Franklin v. Margay Oil Corp.,*
    194 Okla. 519, 153 P.2d 486 (1944) (an Oklahoma statute regulating allocation of oil
    royalties could not constitutionally be applied retroactively). *See* Scott, *Principal or
    Income?,* 100 TRUSTS & EST. 180, 251 (1961); BOGERT, THE LAW OF TRUSTS
    AND TRUSTEES § 847 (2d ed. 1962).
24. UNIFORM MANAGEMENT OF INSTITUTIONAL FUNDS ACT § 6.
25. CAL. CIV. CODE § 2290.6 (1973).
26. UNIFORM MANAGEMENT OF INSTITUTIONAL FUNDS ACT § 4.

27. *Id.* at § 5.
28. *Id.* at § 7.
29. *Id.* at § 7(b).
30. CAL. CIV. CODE §§ 2290.1 through 2290.12 (1973).
31. COLO. REV. STAT. ANN. §§ 31-26-1 through 31-26-9 (1963), *as amended*, H. BILL NO. 1006 (1973).
32. CONN. PUB. ACT NO. 73-548 (1973).
33. ILL. PUB. ACT NO. 78-866 (1973).
34. KANS. H. BILL NO. 1050 (1973).
35. ME. REV. STAT. ANN. tit. 13, ch. 95 (1964), *as amended*, PUB. LAW ch. 286 (1973).
36. MD. ANN. CODE art. 49A, §§ 6-15 (Supp. 1973).
37. MINN. PUB. LAWS ch. 313 (1973).
38. N.H. REV. STAT. ANN. ch. 292-B (Supp. 1973).
39. TENN. PUB. LAWS ch. 177 (1973).
40. VT. STAT. ANN. tit. 14, §§ 3401-07 (Supp. 1973).
41. VA. CODE ANN. §§ 55-268.1 through 55-268.10 (Supp. 1973).
42. WASH. REV. CODE tit. 24 (1969), *as amended*, S. BILL NO. 2081 (1973).
43. MASS. S. BILL NO. 225 (1972); *see* MASS. H. BILL NO. 6159 (1972).
44. MICH. S. BILL NO. 134 (Feb. 14, 1973).
45. MO. H. BILL NO. 1204 (1974).
46. N.J. A. BILL NO. 2484 (Apr. 30, 1973).
47. OHIO S. BILL NO. 386 (1973).
48. WIS. S. BILL NO. 557 (May 10, 1973).
49. R.I. GEN. LAWS ANN. §§ 18-12-1 through 18-12-9 (Supp. 1972).
50. *Compare id.* at § 18-12-1.E *with* UNIFORM MANAGEMENT OF INSTITUTIONAL FUNDS ACT § 1(5).
51. R.I. GEN. LAWS ANN. § 18-12-7 (Supp. 1972).
52. N.Y. NOT-FOR-PROFIT CORP. LAW § 513 (McKinney 1970).
53. *Id.* at § 103 (McKinney Supp. 1972).
54. *Id.* at § 513(d) (McKinney 1970).
55. CARY & BRIGHT, THE LAW AND THE LORE OF ENDOWMENT FUNDS 34-35 (1969).
56. N.Y. NOT-FOR-PROFIT CORP. LAW § 513(e) (McKinney Supp. 1972).
57. PA. CONS. STAT. tit. 15, § 7550(c)(1) (1970), *as amended*, S. BILL NO. 891 (Printer's No. 2116) (1972).
58. *Id.* at § 7550(c)(2).
59. *Id.* at § 7550(d).
60. *Id.* at § 7550(e).
61. *Id.* at § 7551.
62. *Id.* at § 7551(c).
63. N.C. GEN. STAT. § 116-36(f) (1966), *as amended*, H. BILL NO. 1456 (1971).
64. CAL. CORP. CODE § 10251(c) (West Supp. 1973).
65. N.J. REV. STAT. § 15:18-8 (Supp. 1973).
66. *Id.* at § 15:18-11.
67. *Id.* at § 15:18-8.
68. *Id.* at § 15:18-10.
69. *See, e.g.,* ELLIS, INSTITUTIONAL INVESTING 4-5 (1971); Heimann, *The Peterson Commission Report,* and Murray, *Foundation Investments: Problems of Investment Policy,* 10 CONFERENCE ON CHARITABLE FOUNDATIONS, N.Y.U. INST. ON FED. TAX. 19, 29 (1971); ADVISORY COMMITTEE, *supra* note 5, at 26.
70. Miller, *Trustee Responsibility: A Panel Discussion,* 2 MANAGING ENDOWMENT CAPITAL 98, 101 (1970); ELLIS, *supra* note 69, at 188.
71. LOUIS HARRIS, *supra* note 3, at 41; Heimann, *supra* note 69.
72. Lesher, *The Non-profit Corporation—A Neglected Stepchild Comes of Age,* 22 BUS. LAW. 951, 972 (1967).
73. LOUIS HARRIS, *supra* note 3, at 41.
74. *Ibid.*
75. Conard, *Functions of Directors under the Existing System,* 27 BUS. LAW. 23, 24 (1972); *see* MACE, DIRECTORS: MYTH AND REALITY 13-15, 43-48 (1971).
76. Ellis, *Let's Solve the Endowment Crisis,* 48 HARV. BUS. REV., Mar.-Apr. 1970, at 92, 99.
77. *See, e.g.,* ELLIS, *supra* note 69, at 12-17, 192.
78. *Id.* at 17; Murray, *supra* note 69.
79. ADVISORY COMMITTEE, *supra* note 5, at 26.
80. *See* Meck, *Working With Your Investment Manager,* 1 MANAGING ENDOWMENT CAPITAL 75, 79 (1969).
81. ADVISORY COMMITTEE, *supra* note 5, at 49.

82. *Cf.* BOGERT, THE LAW OF TRUSTS AND TRUSTEES § 555 (2d ed. 1960).
83. *Report of the Treasurer of Yale University, 1966-67,* 22-23 (Jan. 27, 1968).
84. LOUIS HARRIS, *supra* note 3, at 48-49.
85. Davidson, *Investing College Endowment Funds: A Comparison of Internal and External Management,* 27 FINANCIAL ANAL. J., Jan.-Feb. 1971, at 72; LOUIS HARRIS, *supra* note 3, at 29.
86. *See, e.g.,* Murray, *supra* note 69, at 32.
87. Karst, *The Efficiency of the Charitable Dollar: An Unfulfilled State Responsibility,* 73 HARV. L. REV. 433, 435-36 (1960).
88. *Meck v. Behrens,* 141 Wash. 676, 685, 252 P. 91, 95 (1927).
89. *Ex parte Belchier,* Ambler 218, 219 (Ch. 1754).
90. *See, e.g.,* Note, *Liability of the Trustee for the Acts of His Delegate,* 52 DICK. L. REV. 255, 257-58 (1948); BOGERT, *supra* note 82, at § 557.
91. RESTATEMENT (SECOND) OF TRUSTS § 225 (1959).
92. RESTATEMENT (SECOND) OF AGENCY § 18, comment c (1958); BOGERT, *supra* note 82, at § 555; 2 FLETCHER, CYCLOPEDIA OF THE LAW OF PRIVATE CORPORATIONS § 268 (rev. vol. 1969).
93. 2 SCOTT, LAW OF TRUSTS § 171.4 (3d ed. 1967).
94. *Chicago Title & Trust Co. v. Zinser,* 264 Ill. 31, 35, 105 N.E. 718, 719 (1914).
95. Note, *Delegation of Duties by Corporate Directors,* 47 VA. L. REV. 278, 279-80 (1961); 6 CAVITCH, BUSINESS ORGANIZATIONS § 126.02[2] (1973).
96. Note, *Delegation of Duties by Corporate Directors,* 47 VA. L. REV. 278, 281 (1961); 6 CAVITCH, *supra* note 95, at § 126.02[2].
97. 6 CAVITCH, *supra* note 95, at § 126.02[2].
98. *See* 1 HORNSTEIN, CORPORATION LAW AND PRACTICE § 420 (1959); Goel, *Delegation of Directors' Powers and Duties—A Comparative Analysis,* 18 INT'L & COMP. L.Q. 152, 153 (1969).
99. BALLANTINE, CORPORATIONS 133 (rev. ed. 1946).
100. *Adams v. Clearance Corp.,* 35 Del. Ch. 318, 322, 116 A.2d 893, 895 (1955), *aff'd,* 35 Del. Ch. 459, 121 A.2d 302 (1956).
101. BALLANTINE, CORPORATIONS 132 (rev. ed. 1946).
102. 2 FLETCHER, *supra* note 92, at § 495; *accord, San Antonio Land Bank v. Taylor,* 129 Tex. 335, 341, 105 S.W.2d 650, 654 (1937); Note, *Delegation of Duties by Corporate Directors,* 47 VA. L. REV. 278, 281 (1961); 29 MICH. L. REV. 367 (1931).
103. RESTATEMENT (SECOND) OF TRUSTS § 379, comment b (1959).
104. MODEL NON-PROFIT CORPORATION ACT § 5 (rev. act 1964).
105. *See, e.g.,* ALA. CODE tit. 10, § 223 (1959); ILL. ANN. STAT. ch. 32 § 163a 20 (Smith-Hurd 1970); IND. ANN. STAT. § 23-7-1.1-10 (Code ed. 1972); MD. CODE ANN. art. 23 § 59 (1957); MO. REV. STAT. § 355.155 (1969); NEB. REV. STAT. § 21-1920 (1970); TEX. REV. CIV. STAT. ANN. art. 1396-2.18 (Supp. 1973); *see* 1 HORNSTEIN, *supra* note 98, at § 512.
106. CAL. CORP. CODE § 10204 (West 1955); TENN. CODE ANN. § 48-1108 (1964).
107. UNIFORM MANAGEMENT OF INSTITUTIONAL FUNDS ACT § 5.
108. *Boston v. Curley,* 276 Mass. 549, 177 N.E. 557 (1931).
109. *Id.* at 551, 177 N.E. at 557.
110. *Id.* at 561-62, 177 N.E. at 562.
111. *Id.* at 562, 177 N.E. at 562.
112. *Id.* at 555, 177 N.E. at 559.
113. *Id.* at 562-63, 177 N.E. at 562.
114. *New England Trust Co. v. Paine,* 317 Mass. 542, 59 N.E.2d 263 (1945).
115. *Id.* at 556, 59 N.E.2d at 272.
116. *Id.* at 557, 59 N.E.2d at 273.
117. *Massachusetts Charitable Mechanic Ass'n v. Beede,* 320 Mass. 601, 70 N.E.2d 825 (1947).
118. *Id.* at 611, 70 N.E.2d at 831.
119. *City of Bangor v. Beal,* 85 Me. 129, 26 A. 1112 (1892).
120. *Wilstach Estate,* 1 Pa. D.&C.2d 197, 213 (Orphans' Ct. 1954).
121. *Id.* at 214.
122. *Graham Bros. Co. v. Galloway Woman's College,* 190 Ark. 692, 81 S.W.2d 837 (1935).
123. UNIFORM MANAGEMENT OF INSTITUTIONAL FUNDS ACT § 5(2).
124. N.Y. NOT-FOR-PROFIT CORP. LAW § 514 (McKinney 1970); PA. CONS. STAT. tit. 15, § 7551 (1970), *as amended,* S. BILL NO. 891 (Printer's No. 2116) (1972).
125. CAL. CORP. CODE § 10204 (West 1955).
126. LA. REV. STAT. §§ 17:2231, 17:2232 (1963).
127. *Murdoch v. Elliot,* 77 Conn. 247, 58 A. 718 (Sup. Ct. Err. 1904).
128. 12 MASS. ATT'Y GEN. REP. 75 (1933).
129. *Attorney Gen. v. Olson,* 346 Mass. 190, 197, 191 N.E.2d 132, 136 (1963).

54

130. *Denckla v. Independence Fnd.*, 41 Del. Ch. 247, 251, 193 A.2d 538, 541 (1963).
131. *Id.* at 252, 193 A.2d at 541.
132. *Id.* at 256, 193 A.2d at 544.
133. *Hospital & Benevolent Ass'n v. Arkansas Baptist State Conv.*, 176 Ark. 946, 958, 4 S.W.2d 933, 937 (1928).
134. *Central Univ. v. Walters' Ex'rs*, 122 Ky. 65, 83, 90 S.W. 1066, 1070 (1906).
135. *E.g., People v. President & Trustees of the College of Cal.*, 38 Cal. 166 (1869); *Holden Hosp. Corp. v. Southern Illinois Hosp. Corp.*, 22 Ill. 2d 150, 174 N.E.2d 793 (1961); *Trustees of Rush Med. College v. University of Chicago*, 312 Ill. 109, 143 N.E. 434 (1924); *Orleans Parish School Bd. v. New Orleans*, 90 So. 2d 683 (La. 1956); *contra, Hempstead v. Meadville Theological School*, 284 Pa. 147, 130 A. 421 (1925).
136. *E.g., Matter of Syracuse Univ. (Heffron)*, 3 N.Y.2d 665, 148 N.E.2d 671, 171 N.Y.S.2d 545 (1958).
137. *E.g., Trevathan v. Ringgold-Noland Fnd.*, 241 Ark. 758, 410 S.W.2d 132 (1967); *Lupton v. Leander Clark College*, 194 Iowa 1008, 187 N.W. 496 (1922); *President and Trustees of Harvard College v. Soc'y for Promoting Theological Ed.*, 69 Mass. (3 Gray) 280 (1855); *Catron v. Scarritt Collegiate Inst.*, 264 Mo. 713, 175 S.W. 571 (1915); *Bible Readers' Aid Soc'y v. Katzenbach*, 97 N.J. Eq. 416, 128 A. 628 (Ch. 1925); *Fenn College v. Nance*, 4 Ohio Misc. 183, 210 N.E.2d 418 (C.P. Cuyahoga County 1965); *cf. Stone v. Inhabitants of Framingham*, 109 Mass. 303 (1872).
138. *Forsyth v. Woods*, 78 U.S. (11 Wall.) 484, 487 (1871).
139. NEWMAN, LAW OF TRUSTS 355 (1949); *accord, e.g.,* RESTATEMENT (SECOND) OF TRUSTS § 171, comment h (1959); 2 SCOTT, LAW OF TRUSTS § 171.2 (3d ed. 1967).
140. *Opinion of the Justices*, 306 A.2d 55, 57 (N.H. 1973).
141. Fratcher, *Trustees' Powers Legislation*, 37 N.Y.U.L. REV. 627, 640 (1962).
142. *Id.* at 658-59.
143. Trustee Act of 1925, 15+16 Geo. 5, c. 19, § 23.
144. *See* Jones, *Delegation by Trustees: A Reappraisal*, 22 MOD. L. REV. 381 (1959); Fratcher, *supra* note 141, at 640-41; 2 SCOTT, LAW OF TRUSTS § 171.2 (3d ed. 1967).
145. Shattuck, *The Development of the Prudent Man Rule for Fiduciary Investment in the United States in the Twentieth Century*, 12 OHIO ST. L.J. 491, 495 (1951).
146. RESTATEMENT (SECOND) OF TRUSTS § 227, comment n (1959); Dillon, *May Trustees Invest in Investment Trusts?*, 89 TRUSTS & EST. 396 (1950).
147. RESTATEMENT (SECOND) OF AGENCY § 18 (1958).
148. *See* BOGERT, *supra* note 82, at § 555.
149. RESTATEMENT (SECOND) OF TRUSTS § 171 (1959).
150. *Id.* at § 171, comment d.
151. *See, e.g., O'Reilly's Estate*, 11 Pa. D.&C. 549 (Phil. Co. 1929); 2 SCOTT, LAW OF TRUSTS § 171.2 (3d ed. 1967); *cf. Attorney Gen. v. Olson*, 346 Mass. 190, 197, 191 N.E.2d 132, 136 (1963).
152. *In re Estate of Rosenthal*, 189 So. 2d 507 (Fla. App. 1966).
153. BOGERT, *supra* note 82, at § 555.
154. *Speight v. Gaunt*, 22 Ch. Div. 727, 739-40 (Ct. of App.), *aff'd*, 9 App. Cas. 1 (H.L.) (1883).
155. *Dodge v. Stickney*, 62 N.H. 330, 337 (1882).
156. *Schofield v. Cleveland Trust Co.*, 24 Ohio Op. 345 (C.P. 1942), *aff'd*, 47 Ohio L. Abs. 321, 72 N.E.2d 122 (Ct. App. 1947), *modified*, 149 Ohio St. 133, 78 N.E.2d 167 (1948).
157. *Anderson v. Roberts*, 147 Mo. 486, 493-95, 48 S.W. 847, 848 (1898).
158. 15 U.S.C.A. § 80a (1971).
159. *Id.* at § 80a-15.
160. 6 CAVITCH, *supra* note 95, at § 126.03; CARY, CORPORATIONS 221 (4th ed. 1969).
161. 6 CAVITCH, *supra* note 95, at § 126.03.
162. *Dyer Bros. Golden West Iron Works v. Central Iron Works*, 182 Cal. 588, 594, 189 P. 445, 447-48 (1920).
163. *McCord v. Thompson-Starrett Co.*, 129 App. Div. 130, 113 N.Y.S. 385 (1st Dep't 1908), *aff'd*, 198 N.Y. 587, 92 N.E. 1090 (1910).
164. *Cullen v. Governor Clinton Co.*, 279 App. Div. 483, 485, 110 N.Y.S.2d 614, 616 (1st Dep't 1952).
165. *William Sellers & Co. v. Clarke-Harrison, Inc.*, 354 Pa. 109, 118, 46 A.2d 497, 501 (1946).
166. *Kelly v. Bell*, 254 A.2d 62, 72 (Del. Ch. 1969), *aff'd*, 266 A.2d 878 (Del. 1970).
167. *Ray v. Homewood Hospital, Inc.*, 223 Minn. 440, 444, 27 N.W.2d 409, 411 (1947).
168. *Lane v. Bogert*, 116 N.J. Eq. 454, 174 A. 217 (Ch. 1934); 6 CAVITCH, *supra* note 95, at § 126.02[2]; Note, *Delegation of Duties by Corporate Directors*, 47 VA. L. REV. 278, 289-90 (1961).
169. *Kennerson v. Burbank Amusement Co.*, 120 Cal. App. 2d 157, 173, 260 P.2d 823, 832-33 (1953).

170. *See, e.g., Sherman & Ellis, Inc. v. Indiana Mut. Cas. Co.*, 41 F.2d 588 (7th Cir.), *cert. denied*, 282 U.S. 893 (1930) (striking down a 20-year management contract); *Shaw v. Bankers' National Life Ins. Co.*, 61 Ind. App. 346, 112 N.E. 16 (1916) (striking down a 30-year management contract).

171. Cases invalidating purported attempts to delegate most of the functions of corporate boards of directors include *Sherman & Ellis, Inc. v. Indiana Mut. Cas. Co., supra* note 170; *Kennerson v. Burbank Amusement Co., supra* note 169; *Royal Theatre Corp. v. United States*, 66 F. Supp. 301 (D. Kan. 1946) (tax case; delegation not central issue); *Wheeler v. Layman Fnd.*, 188 Ga. 267, 3 S.E.2d 645 (1939); *Long Park, Inc. v. Trenton-New Brunswick Theatres Co.*, 297 N.Y. 174, 77 N.E.2d 633 (1948); *Knickerbocker Investment Co. v. Voorhees*, 100 App. Div. 414, 91 N.Y. Supp. 816 (1st Dep't 1905). Cases upholding such delegation include *Adams v. Clearance Corp.*, 35 Del. Ch. 318, 116 A.2d 893 (1955), *aff'd*, 35 Del. Ch. 459, 121 A.2d 302 (1956); *Kidd v. New Hampshire Traction Co.*, 74 N.H. 160, 66 A. 127 (1907); *Lorillard v. Clyde*, 86 N.Y. 384 (1881); *William Sellers & Co. v. Clarke-Harrison, Inc.*, 354 Pa. 109, 46 A.2d 497 (1946).

172. BALLANTINE, CORPORATIONS 136 (rev. ed. 1946); 6 CAVITCH, *supra* note 95, at § 126.03; Goel, *Delegation of Directors' Powers and Duties—A Comparative Analysis*, 18 INT'L & COMP. L.Q. 152, 170-72 (1969)

173. *E.g., West v. Camden*, 135 U.S. 507 (1890); *Trumbo v. Bank of Berkeley*, 77 Cal. App. 2d 704, 176 P.2d 376 (1947); *Jacobson v. Barnes*, 176 Minn. 4, 222 N.W. 341 (1928); *Tremsky v. Green*, 106 N.Y.S.2d 572 (Sup. Ct. 1951); *but see Streett v. Laclede-Christy Co.*, 409 S.W.2d 691 (Mo. 1966); *Clark v. Dodge*, 269 N.Y. 410, 199 N.E. 641 (1936); *Overseas Raw Materials Corp v. Coster*, 285 App. Div. 1021, 139 N.Y.S.2d 718 (1st Dep't 1955).

174. 2 FLETCHER, *supra* note 92, at § 501.

175. 2 SCOTT, LAW OF TRUSTS § 171.2 (3d ed. 1967).

176. *Bohlen's Estate*, 75 Pa. 304, 317-18 (1874).

177. *In re Kohler's Estate*, 348 Pa. 55, 56-57, 33 A.2d 920, 921 (1943).

178. *Id.* at 59, 33 A.2d at 922-23.

179. *Newton v. Bronson*, 13 N.Y. 587, 594-95 (1856).

180. *E.g., Hill v. Peoples*, 80 Ark. 15, 95 S.W. 990 (1906); *Duncan v. Kahn*, 151 Cal. App. 2d 402, 311 P.2d 587 (Dist. Ct. of App. 1957); *Munn v. Burges*, 70 Ill. 604 (1873); *Hawley v. James*, 5 Paige 318 (1835), *modified on other grounds*, 16 Wend. 61 (N.Y. 1836); *Parker v. Banks*, 79 N.C. 480 (1878); *contra, Clevenger v. Rio Farms, Inc.*, 204 S.W.2d 40 (Tex. App. 1947).

181. *Cf. New England Trust Co. v. Paine*, 317 Mass. 542, 556, 59 N.E.2d 263, 272 (1945).

182. ADVISORY COMMITTEE, *supra* note 5, at xi.